SOUTH TO THE
GREAT STEPPE

First published in 2015, in the United Kingdom by:
FIRST, Victory House, 99-10 Regent Street,
London, W1B 4EZ, United Kingdom.

ISBN: 978-0-9546409-9-6
Published in the United Kingdom

Cover image: *A bard entertains a group of Kazakhs on The Steppe*

The publishers would like to acknowledge the assistance of
HE Erzhan Kazykhanov, Ambassador of the Republic of Kazakhstan to the
Court of St James', Samruk-Kazyna and the British-Kazakh Society.

THE QUEEN'S AWARDS
FOR ENTERPRISE
2013

FIRST

Victory House, 99-10 Regent Street, London, W1B 4EZ, United Kingdom
Tel: +44 20 7440 3500 Fax: +44 20 7440 3544 Email: publisher@firstmagazine.com
URL: www.firstmagazine.com

SOUTH TO THE GREAT STEPPE

The travels of Thomas and Lucy Atkinson
in Eastern Kazakhstan, 1847–1852

BY NICK FIELDING

The publishers wish to acknowledge
the assistance and support of
Samruk-Kazyna
in the preparation of this book.

Produced in association with:

The British-Kazakh Society

Contents

Foreword

It gives me great pleasure to introduce *South to the Great Steppe*, a landmark book which describes the journeys of Thomas Witlam Atkinson and his wife Lucy, across lands which now form part of present day Kazakhstan. This story of British 19th Century exploration in the most remote areas of the Great Steppe is vividly brought to life by Nick Fielding, who has himself retraced part of this epic journey, on horseback, with his own wife Rosamund.

This book is important for all those interested in Central Asia – and especially Kazakhstan. With its strategic geographic location and dominant position in the region, modern Kazakhstan has developed a key international role, generating considerable attention. I first visited Kazakhstan shortly after independence in 1991 and have had a chance to witness the country's many significant changes and achievements.

President Nursultan Nazarbayev is the architect of his country's success and the transformation which he has overseen has brought dramatic improvements to the lives of the Kazakhstani people. Today Kazakhstan is distinguished by its strong sense of national identity, multi-ethnic harmony and political stability.

South to the Great Steppe provides important insights and background to Kazakhstan's cultural, historical and geographical identity. It also demonstrates the longstanding links, and shared history, between Kazakhstan and the United Kingdom. *South to the Great Steppe* helps place this bilateral relationship in its historical context.

Given the British-Kazakh Society's central role in promoting the best of relations between Britain and Kazakhstan by fostering mutual cooperation and understanding – I am delighted the Society is so closely associated with this important book.

I am especially grateful to HE Erzhan Kazykhanov, Kazakhstan's Ambassador, and his staff for their vital help and guidance in the preparation of *South to the Great Steppe*. We are also grateful to the National Welfare Fund of Kazakhstan – Samruk Kazyna – for providing grant funding to enable this cultural history to be brought to the widest possible audience.

South to the Great Steppe is a tribute to Nick Fielding's meticulous research and dedicated scholarship. We are grateful to him for shining such a well-focused light on the shared history of our two countries.

We at FIRST are delighted to have been asked to produce such an important cultural and historical work and hope that *South to the Great Steppe* contributes to even greater understanding of Kazakhstan's remarkable people, culture and landscapes. ■

Rupert Goodman FRGS DL
Chairman, British-Kazakh Society
Chairman and Founder, FIRST

Preface

Strange as it may seem, my decision to write about the remarkable lives of Thomas and Lucy Atkinson grew, in the first instance, out of my interest in Central Asian textiles. More than 20 years ago, in an effort to understand the complex movements of peoples and cultures behind the spread of textile patterns, I first began to travel in this and neighbouring regions. Those travels have since taken me right across Central Asia, into Mongolia and southern Siberia, increasingly focussed on the subjects of this book.

So it was that I first came across the writings of Thomas Witlam Atkinson. I was surprised to find that a man who had written so extensively and in such detail about what was once called Oriental Siberia or Western Tartary was so little known in the modern era. Thomas' descriptions of life on what we would now call the Kazakh steppes, and onward into remote parts of Xinjiang, Mongolia and southern Siberia, are unique. Although others passed through these lands, few spent any time in these largely unknown territories. Thomas and his wife Lucy – who also penned a remarkable book describing their travels - spent almost seven years in this vast region, travelling tens of thousands of miles. Even more amazingly, Lucy gave birth to a son in Kapal, a tiny town that was then the most remote outpost of the Russian Empire.

It has taken me several years to sort out all the many complexities of this amazing story. In 2015 alone I have travelled to Hawaii, to Kazakhstan and to Krasnoyarsk in Siberia in pursuit of the Atkinsons. Even though I have spent my professional life working as an investigative journalist, the twists and turns in the narrative have sometimes come close to defeating me. And still, of course, there are gaps in our knowledge that are waiting to be filled. I feel sure that archives in Russia and Kazakhstan still hold some fascinating details about the Atkinsons. Why they became so obscure and little known is still a mystery. Hopefully this book will begin the process of restoring them to the position they so richly deserve. ∎

Nick Fielding
Oxford

Chapter
ONE
INTRODUCTION

In the summer of 1846, a rather unusual Englishman arrived in the Russian Imperial capital of St Petersburg. Well into his middle years, a little down at heel, but with an open face and an uncanny ability to get on with almost anyone, Thomas Witlam Atkinson was at a turning point. For the previous six or seven years his life had been in turmoil, but now he had hit upon a plan. A stonemason turned architect, with a string of remarkable neo-Gothic buildings and churches to his name, he was now about to embark on a new journey in his life. After living abroad for the previous four years and facing up to the tragic death of his son, he had decided to travel to some of the most remote areas on Earth – Siberia, Central Asia, Mongolia and northern China – armed with little more than a sketchbook. The architect had become the artist.

"My sole object was to sketch the scenery of Siberia – scarcely at all known to Europeans," he wrote in the preface to his first book, *Oriental and Western Siberia: a narrative of seven years'*

Explorations and Adventures[1]. *"While thus employed, I passed out of the Emperor of Russia's Asiatic dominions; having been provided with an especial passport by command of His Imperial Majesty, Nicholas the First, which enabled me to cross the frontier, as well as to re-enter the Empire at any other points to which my rambles might lead me."*

What prompted this practical Yorkshireman, born in 1799 in the small south Yorkshire village of Cawthorne, near Barnsley, to set off for such remote destinations as he approached his half-century? He was not an explorer by background and until 1842 at least had had a comparatively sheltered life, with no evidence that he had ever left the British Isles.

Nor was that the only remarkable thing about Thomas Atkinson. Soon after arriving in St Petersburg Thomas was to meet Lucy Sherrard Finley, a young, well-educated English governess, employed by one of the grandest families in the Imperial capital, with direct connections to the heart of the Russian aristocracy. Lucy was 29 and unmarried. From a Dissenting background, her family originated from the north-east of England where they had been involved in the Baltic trade for many years, running trading ships between St Petersburg and England in the summer and then over the Channel to France during the winter.

At some point during the latter part of 1846, as he made his way around the salons of Imperial St Petersburg, Thomas and Lucy fell in love. But it was not simple. He was about begin a journey eastwards that was scheduled to last for several years. In the mid-nineteenth century much of the region between the Urals and the Pacific Ocean almost five thousand miles away was unknown, not to mention dangerous, inhabited by wild tribesmen and subject to greater variations in temperature than almost anywhere on earth.

Undoubtedly Thomas soon appreciated the advantages that would come from a relationship with Lucy. She spoke fluent Russian, whereas he did not. She was in the employ of a general in the Imperial Army who was also president of the Russian Geographical Society. And despite his loyalty to the Emperor, General Muravyev-Vilensky was a scion of a family that had wholeheartedly thrown itself behind the reformers who supported the Decembrist uprising against the Tsars in 1825. One of his cousins had been executed and others sentenced to a life of exile in Siberia. Yet another cousin was the Governor of Eastern Siberia. Lucy's connections to this remarkable family were to prove crucial to the success of their travels. The marriage of Thomas and Lucy in the winter of 1848 in Moscow proved to be full of surprises.

But for now, Thomas, armed with a letter of introduction from John Fane, the Earl of Westmorland and British Envoy Extraordinary and Minister Plenipotentiary to Prussia, was intent on gaining permission for a journey he hoped would make his reputation as an artist. His first port of call was the British Legation in St Petersburg, where he was soon able to win over the British Minister Plenipotentiary to Russia, Andrew Buchanan. Records in the Bodleian Library include a letter from Buchanan to his superior in London, the future prime minister, Viscount Palmerston, dated October 1846:

By kind permission of Paul Dahlquist

The only known photograph of Thomas Atkinson,
taken shortly before he died in 1861

" *Mr Atkinson, an English artist, who was recommended to the protection of Her Majesty's Legation by the Earl of Westmorland, requested me some time ago to employ my good offices with Count Nesselrode (the Russian Foreign Minister), with the view to obtain the sanction of the Emperor to a professional tour which he proposes making in Siberia and the Altai, and I am happy to say that, in consequence of his Imperial Majesty's orders, every facility has been afforded to Mr Atkinson by the Imperial authorities for the completion of his purpose. Mr Atkinson will be accompanied by an Englishman who has been for some time residing in this country. They will visit Kiachta and intend to penetrate as far as possible into China. I have therefore called Mr Atkinson's attention to several points of political and commercial interest on which Her Majesty's Government might be glad to receive information and he has promised to bear them in mind and report upon them to Her Majesty's Legation on his return to St Petersburgh. I have the honour to be, with the highest respect, My Lord, Your Lordship's Most Obedient, Humble Servant, Andrew Buchanan*"[2].

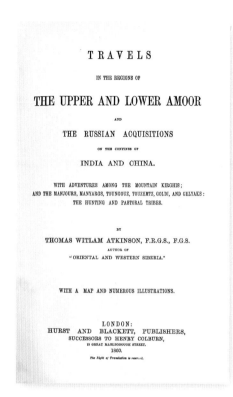
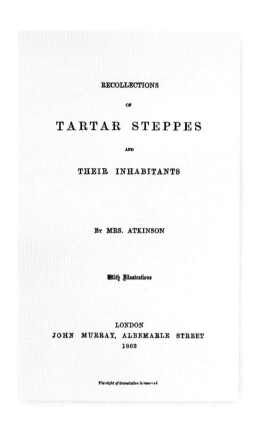

The title pages to the books by Thomas and Lucy Atkinson

Buchanan was not exaggerating when he said that "every facility had been afforded to Mr Atkinson" by the Russian authorities. The terms of the *ukase* (passport) granted to Thomas meant that he was entitled to receive transport – carriages, sledges, horses, boats or whatever was available – provisions, Cossack protection and guides – at any of the post-houses along his route entirely at the expense of his hosts. He was required to pay nothing in return. Over the course of nearly seven years, travelling a total of 40,000 miles, Thomas' expenditure was almost nil. *"I am deeply indebted to the late Emperor of Russia, for without his passport I should have been stopped at every government, and insurmountable difficulties would have been thrown in my way. This slip of paper proved a talisman wherever presented in his dominions and swept down every obstacle raised to bar my progress,"* is how Thomas described the importance of the document issued to him personally by Tsar Nicholas I.

It was a remarkable coup for an Englishman, at a time when tensions between Britain and imperial Russia were growing by the day. By 1854, only months after Thomas and Lucy – along with their son, Alatau, born during the course of their travels – returned to St Petersburg at the end of their wanderings, the two countries were at war with each other in the Crimea. Not until 1856 did Thomas venture back to England, to arrange the publication of his first book, which appeared two years later. That was followed by a further volume in 1860[3], with a third volume planned, but which never appeared due to Thomas's untimely death in July 1861. Three years later Lucy also published a book, *Recollections of Tartar Steppes*[4], which is all the more remarkable for being one of the earliest travel books written ever written by a woman.

All three books describe the incredible journeys made by the Atkinsons, surely the greatest husband-and-wife travellers of all time. And yet today, their names are barely known. Neither Thomas nor Lucy have received the plaudits they so richly deserve. This book marks the beginning of an effort to correct that injustice. It will concentrate on the journeys Thomas and Lucy made into Central Asia, in particular to what is today eastern Kazakhstan, known in the mid-nineteenth century as Oriental Tartary, the Kirghis (more properly Kazakh) Steppes and Chinese Tartary.

This first attempt at a biography of the Atkinsons is limited in scope, discussing only the first two or three years of their travels into the vastness of the Central Asian steppes, in an area that is today located largely in Kazakhstan. Until it was conquered by the Russians – a process that lasted the best part of 40 years in the second half of the nineteenth century – Central Asia was made up of a number of independent khanates. Bokhara, Khokan, Samarkand, Merv and others were the fiefdoms of numerous petty princes and tyrants. Thomas' arrival in Russia coincided with the first efforts by Russia to seize the northern steppes that stretched all the way from the Urals to China and to attempt to bring some kind of control to this wide region.

As Thomas declared in the introduction to *Oriental and Western Siberia*:

"*Neither the old Venetian[5] nor the Jesuit priests could have visited these regions – their travels having been far to the south; nor am I aware that they brought back any pictorial representations of the scenes through which they wandered. Even the recent travellers, Huc and Gabet[6], who visited 'the land of grass' (the plains to the south of the great Desert of Gobi,) did not penetrate into the country of the Kalkas; and the illustrations to their works were evidently fabricated in Paris.*"

In contrast, Thomas made three substantial journeys into Central Asia, on the second one of which – by far the longest – he was accompanied by Lucy. Using copies of Thomas's own watercolours and sketches – he brought back to England more than 560 sketches and completed watercolours of his travels, together with modern-day photographs and other illustrations, this book will tell the story of those three journeys. The Atkinsons were certainly the earliest European visitors to much of eastern Kazakhstan and their writings offer us a unique window into conditions and life on the steppes at this time. They met many of the leading khans and sultans on their journey, offering us tantalising glimpses into a way of life that has long since disappeared. Their accounts provide some of the only descriptions of the people and places that existed prior to the arrival of the Russians.

And they were witnesses to history. As the Russians sent a Cossack expeditionary force of around 500 men south in the summer of 1848, along the line of the Tien Shan Mountains which marked the border with the Celestial Chinese Empire, Thomas and Lucy were only a few weeks behind, residing in their most southerly and remote bastion at Kapal for almost nine months. That was where in November 1848 Lucy gave birth to their son, named Alatau Tamchiboulac Atkinson, after the nearby mountain range and a sacred spring on the steppes close to the base of the mountains. This, then, is the epic story of Thomas and Lucy Atkinson's pioneering journeys into the Kazakh Steppes, then one of the remotest points on earth. ∎

1. Thomas Witlam Atkinson, *Oriental and Western Siberia: a narrative of seven years' Explorations and Adventures*, Hurst and Blackett, London, 1858.

2. British Embassy, St. Petersburg, Manuscript volumes, British Library, CLI Add MS 48567, June 1846-7.

3. Thomas Witlam Atkinson, *Travels in the Regions of the Upper and Lower Amoor*, Hurst and Blackett, London, 1860.

4. *Mrs Lucy Atkinson, Recollections of Tartar Steppes*, John Murray, London, 1863.

5. *Marco Polo*

6. Abbé Évariste Huc and Abbé Joseph Gabet were French Catholic missionaries who travelled extensively in Central Asia and particularly Tibet in the 1840s.

The ornate cover of Thomas Atkinson's first book,
Oriental and Western Siberia

Chapter
TWO

THE ARCHITECT BECOMES ARTIST

Thomas Atkinson was not the most obvious candidate for a nineteenth century explorer. Very much a practical man, he had neither money, nor education, nor connections, having been brought up as the son of a stonemason in Yorkshire. His father William was head mason at Cannon Hall, the grand home of the Spencer Stanhope family in the village of Cawthorne, a few miles west of Barnsley in south Yorkshire, while his mother Martha was a maid in the house. She was William's second wife – the first, Elizabeth Bates, died in 1795 aged 24 after only three years of marriage, having produced two children.

Little is known about Thomas' early life. He was born in a house adjoining the old Wesleyan chapel in the village and was baptised on 6 March 1799. His baptism is recorded as 'Thomas, son of William and Martha Atkinson – mason'. No mention is made of his middle name Witlam (sometimes Whitlam) which he appears to have added later and which

was his mother's maiden name. Both William and Martha, who married on 19 August 1798, signed their own names in the register, indicating they were literate. From the dates available, it would appear that Martha was already pregnant when she married William.

Thomas attended the village school in Cawthorne but by the time he had reached the age of ten his father would regularly take him from school in the summer months to assist him as a labourer. He continued to attend school during the winter and was able to maintain his studies with the help of his elder brother Charles, the son of his father's first wife, who had been educated at a good school in Sheffield and who gave him lessons in writing and drawing

Thomas' mother Martha died in 1817, when he was only 18. Two years later, aged 20, he married Rebecca Mercer, who was five or six years older than him. The marriage took place

Cannon Hall, home of the Spencer Stanhopes, 1821

on 1 April 1819 in Halifax, which is about 30 miles north-west of Barnsley, on the outskirts of Leeds. There were big stone quarries in Halifax at this time and it is likely that Thomas was working at one of them for a few months. His first child, a daughter called Martha in memory of his mother, was born in Halifax in 1820.

By his early twenties Thomas was employed as a stonecarver at St George's Church in Barnsley. Every day he walked the five miles each-way from Cawthorne to Barnsley and back.

According to the *Dictionary of National Biography*[1] at this time he also worked on a church in Ashton under Lyne about 40 kilometres west of Barnsley on the outskirts of Manchester, where he was briefly employed as a teacher of drawing. He also sculpted a handsome headstone for his mother at All Saints' Church in Cawthorne. Thomas' knowledge of masonry and carving no doubt stood him in good stead for his new

career, which began to expand rapidly, mainly due to the Church Building Act of 1818, whereby the Government had made available a million pounds for the construction of Anglican churches – commonly known as 'Commissioners' churches' or Waterloo churches. This enormous building programme, funded from reparations obtained from France following the defeat of Napoleon at Waterloo, created many new opportunities for Thomas. By 1822 Thomas was working as Clerk of Works to the prominent architect George Basevi on such buildings as the neo-classical St Thomas' Church in Stockport, yet another Commissioners' church.

From 1824-27 Thomas moved on to work at St George's Church, Ramsgate in Kent, where he is recorded as being the surveyor under the architect Henry E Kendall. Slowly but surely Thomas began to make a reputation for himself, but even while he was working away from Yorkshire, he kept in close contact with the Spencer Stanhope family, who were very supportive of

St Nicholas Church, Tooting

the talented young man. In particular, the Reverend Charles Spencer Stanhope, non-resident vicar of the church at Cawthorne and younger brother of John Spencer Stanhope, recognised Atkinson's raw talent and retained a life-long interest in his career and well-being. In November 1860 he accompanied Thomas on a final visit to Cawthorne and was one of the last people to correspond with him before his death in August 1861.

Mrs Pickering, daughter of John Spencer Stanhope, also mentions Thomas in her memoirs: *"At the time of my grandfather's death, he made a design for a tomb for him, which showed so much talent that my uncle Charles sent for him and told him that he had his fortune at his fingers' ends, but not as a mason"*.

The altar tomb, now set in the north chancel chapel, is based on an early Tudor design and has been narrowed and moved from its original position into a recess.

There is another important element of the connection between Thomas and the Spencer Stanhopes. John Spencer Stanhope (1787-1873), who inherited Cannon Hall on the death of his father Walter in 1821, was himself a remarkable man. After studying classics at Cambridge he left England in January 1810 to visit Sicily and Greece en route to those parts of Iberia not occupied by Napoleon's Grand Armée. In a strange twist of fate, after leaving Gibraltar on a small coaster he was treacherously betrayed into French hands in the Spanish port of Barcelona. Narrowly escaping execution, he was later sent to the great fortress at Verdun, and then, eventually, on to Paris. In total he spent more than two-and-a-half years in French custody. Remarkably, he was allowed to spend three months in Paris researching his interests in Greek battlefields, at which point he made the acquaintance of members of the Institut Royal de France. With their support, he obtained permission to continue his travels and research, Napoleon himself ordering Spencer Stanhope's liberty

Eastwood House in Stalybridge, built by Thomas Atkinson for John Cheetham MP

Astley Cheetham Art Collection, Tameside MBC

without condition. His passport can still be seen preserved in the study at Cannon Hall.

Spencer Stanhope returned to England and afterwards in October 1813 travelled through Germany to Greece, this time with his brother Edward Collingwood, where despite serious illness – including a near-fatal attack of malaria – he completed his research. He spent much time measuring and surveying ancient Greek temples and buildings. Using precision instruments, such as the sextant and tape measures, the group were amongst the first to use modern scientific techniques to study the past. They used Herodotus and other classical authors to guide their studies, together with the descriptions made by French consul and antiquarian Louis François Sebastien Fauvel. They were also the first to locate the site of the ancient hippodrome in Olympia.

In 1814 Spencer Stanhope's researches were laid before the Institut Royal in Paris, and in 1817 were published in London under the titles *Topography Illustrative of the Battle of Plataea*, followed in 1824 by *Olympia or Topography illustrative of the actual state of the Plain of Olympia and of the Ruins of the City of Elis* and by *Topographical sketches of Megalopolis, Tanagra, Aulis, and Eretria* in 1831. These three volumes were some of the first attempts at creating what later became the science of archaeology, by measuring buildings accurately and adopting a scientific attitude of inquiry. Stanhope Spencer was elected an Honorary Correspondent of the French Geographical Society and in 1822 a correspondent of the Institut Royal de France. In England he was also elected a Fellow of the Royal Society and of the Society of Antiquaries. The publication of his books places him firmly amongst the philhellenes and their support for Greece's struggle for independence.

Although John was 12 or 13 years older than Thomas, he would have known him all his life. Was he some kind of role model for the young mason? Did the dramatic stories of his capture at sea, imprisonment, release under the personal seal of Napoleon and foreign travel shape Thomas' own outlook? Perhaps Thomas' awareness of the Spencer Stanhopes led him to romanticise travel and adventure and showed him how connections to wealth and influence could be helpful in pursuing personal goals?

According to Worthies of Barnsley[2], this is the case:

"*Atkinson, whose desire for travel had been kindled at an early age by the stirring incidents in the travels of Mr Stanhope when Atkinson was a lad and working on the Cannon Hall estate and his young mind so impressed with the romance of travel by the imprisonments and dangers that had been braved by the young squire (whose return had been signalised by great demonstrations of joy, not only at the Hall, but throughout the village) that his mind was imbued with the idea that to travel to an unknown land was the greatest achievement any man could aspire to. Therefore, when the Emperor of Russia proposed to send him to make surveys in Siberia, he found in Atkinson a most willing servant, as it gave the latter an opportunity of realising the ambition of his life; to emulate or even surpass the researches of his former patron, whose example he followed in giving to the world an account of his explorations.*"

Charles Spencer Stanhope also recognised the quality of the tomb that Thomas had designed for his father and encouraged him to move, first to Manchester and then on to London. Stanhope says that on arriving in London Thomas engaged himself to an architect and continued to study in his spare time, developing a particular interest in Gothic architecture, which was undergoing something of a revival. He began to visit cathedrals and churches, making careful drawings of the stonework.

In 1825 Thomas had still not travelled outside of England, but his expertise as a draughtsman and architect continued to grow. Four years later Thomas published his first book. Written – or more precisely, drawn – jointly with his half-brother Charles, *Gothic Ornament* contains 44 plates drawn from the original carved stonework selected by the two men. The specific pieces of stonework they chose to highlight in the book were from the great cathedrals and churches of England, including Canterbury, Lincoln, Lichfield, Boston and Ely. The book's publication coincided with the growth of the neo-gothic movement led by Augustus Pugin and his son A.W.N. Pugin and demonstrates both the high quality of the Atkinson brothers' draughtsmanship and also their ambition.

By the early 1830s Thomas and Rebecca had three children, Martha, John William (born in Yorkshire in 1825) and Emma,

Hough Hill Priory, Stalybridge, designed by Thomas Atkinson

born in 1830 in Lambeth. The family must have moved to London and stayed for at least three or four years. The same year Thomas exhibited his first work at the Royal Academy – his drawing for the tomb of Walter Spencer Stanhope at Cawthorne. In February that year Thomas had been at the church, along with the Revd. Charles Spencer Stanhope, measuring up for the installation of the newly completed tomb.

Having served his time as a clerk of works, Thomas was able to set himself up as an independent architect in Upper Stamford Street in Southwark, south London. Soon after he was engaged by John Cheetham, MP for South Lancashire, to build a mansion for him at Stalybridge in Cheshire, just outside Manchester. He also built Hough Hill Priory at Stalybridge for John Cheetham's brother, David Cheetham, exhibiting a painting of the building at the Royal Academy in 1832.

The Royal Institute of British Architects holds several of Thomas' original drawings, including a design for a London town house of March 1830 and some of the contract drawings for Hough Hill Priory at Stalybridge. He was still in London in 1832 when he exhibited a drawing of St Nicholas Church, Tooting, another neo-Gothic-styled Commissioners' church, for which he was the architect – and which still stands.

At some point after 1833 Thomas moved back north to Manchester. The 1834 edition of Pigot's Directory gives his address as 25 Piccadilly. The railway had come to Manchester in 1830 and the city was expanding rapidly. He formed a brief partnership with Alfred Bower Clayton who he may have met in London when Clayton was working on the Corn Exchange, Mark Lane (the partnership was dissolved in October 1836). He is also credited as being the architect for St Barnabas Church in Openshaw, Manchester, begun in 1837 (and demolished in 1959).

Perhaps his most ambitious building was the Manchester and Liverpool Bank headquarters in Spring Gardens, Manchester, which was completed in 1834. He also designed and built at least two branch buildings for the bank. Of the bank headquarters in Spring Gardens, *The Builder* later wrote: *"The building of the District Bank was as important an event in the architectural history of Manchester, as that of the Travellers' Club was in London, since it showed the local public that effect was not dependent on mere 'orders', that there was something more than these in the matter of architecture"* .

In addition Thomas built Italianate mansions in the rapidly expanding suburbs for Manchester's increasingly wealthy population. There is a possibility that he was also involved in the rebuilding of the Palace of Westminster, which had been destroyed by a fire in 1834. The Gothic perpendicular style of its replacement, designed by Charles Barry and Augustus W N Pugin, would have suited Thomas perfectly.

By the late 1830s, Thomas' firm was winning some prestigious commissions, including the now partially demolished St Luke's church in Cheetham Hill, Manchester, built in the perpendicular Gothic style which he started in 1836 and which was consecrated in October 1839. The composer Mendelssohn played on the church's magnificent organ for over an hour when he visited the building in April 1847. Nor was Thomas' work confined to Manchester. In 1838 he was looking into the possibility of a major refurbishment project at Markree Castle in Co. Sligo. He built houses at Ashton, at Stockport and in Manchester itself. Again, *The Builder* article already cited is full of praise for him:

"During the few years in which Atkinson practised in Manchester, taste certainly improved by his example. In his Italian villas, bold cantilever cornices and more effective porches and chimneys; and in the Gothic designs, the features which are now well known, but were then habitually caricatured, were introduced; indeed his Gothic was considerably in advance of that practised by London architects. To show the change that has taken place, it may be well to mention that at Atkinson's arrival in Manchester, the architects of the town had their assistants for nearly everything beyond surveying, from London. Most of these assistants had been indebted for what they could do, to one master, the now deceased and too-much forgotten George Maddox of Furnival's Inn: they had not rested long enough in his school to acquire his unquestionable taste; and they were generally deficient in such matters as Gothic mouldings and tracery, to an extent which now seems a deficiency in the power to produce no matter what character of good architecture. By all these gentlemen, some of whom have since deservedly attained a good position, and were then sufficiently qualified to judge, Atkinson was pointed to as a rare bird, a man veritably who made his own designs and was an artist."

Manchester Archives

Manchester Archives

By kind permission of the Royal Bank of Scotland Group plc ©2015

Buildings designed by Thomas Atkinson.
Top: St. George's Church, Ramsgate; Middle: St. Luke's, Cheetham Hill,
and St. Barnabas, Openshaw; Bottom: Manchester and Liverpool Bank.

One of Thomas Atkinsons' illustrations from his book
'Gothic Ornament'

However, despite appearances to the contrary, all was not well. Architecture in the early nineteenth century was a precarious profession. Architects acted as middlemen between suppliers and their commissioning clients and often took a financial risk when ordering supplies and awaiting payment. Details are scant, but Thomas certainly got into financial difficulties.

On 18 May 1838, *The London Gazette* records a bankruptcy petition against Thomas and asks his creditors to attend a meeting in July that year. It is not certain who the petitioner was, although *The Builder* put his indebtedness down to "*a too liberal expenditure on works of art*".

What precisely happened after that is unclear, but by November that year the immediate threat of bankruptcy had been lifted. However, in February 1841 he is listed in the Kings Bench and Fleet Prison Discharge Books as being released on sureties, suggesting that he spent time under lock and key in London – the usual consequence of bankruptcy in those days. His creditors included John Skerrette Stubbs, a fashionable Manchester draper, who had himself been made bankrupt in the mid-1830s. In April 1841 Thomas was again before the Court of Insolvent Debtors in Portugal Street, Lincoln's Inn, as a prisoner. He gives as his address a hotel in London. Perhaps his creditors had forced him to leave Manchester and come to court in London?

Whatever the circumstances of his indebtedness, they did not stop Thomas working and exhibiting. In 1840 he exhibited three works at the Royal Academy, including two views of St Luke's and one of a 'Catholic Church, Manchester', presumably St Mary's, which was rebuilt during this period. By this time Thomas and Rebecca had moved four miles to the south-east of Manchester to Chorlton cum Hardy, a small village with a population of around 700, with a distinctly middle class flavour. While there, on 11 July 1840 in St Clement's church, his eldest daughter Martha married James Wheeler, an up-and-coming solicitor involved in the rapidly expanding railway industry. James' father John Wheeler is described on the marriage certificate as a 'gentleman', which must have greatly pleased the Atkinsons, indicating as it did that their daughter was marrying into society.

Thomas Atkinson's designs for villas in St Luke Place, Smedley

Thomas Atkinson's proposal for an observatory [RIBA]

Thomas' financial problems don't appear to have affected the wedding, although it is likely that the threat of bankruptcy would not have been good for his business. The most likely effect is that it would have been very difficult for him as a discharged bankrupt to obtain credit. Taking on a large building project such as a church, a bank or municipal building would have been impossible without access to credit. One solution may have been for Thomas to take a break for a while by travelling abroad.

There are good grounds for believing this to be the case, as the next we hear of Thomas is through his drawings exhibited at the Royal Academy in June 1842. Surprisingly, they are of the Hazarduari (Palace of a Thousand Doors) Palace at Murshidabad, to the north of Calcutta in West Bengal, India. The Hazarduari Palace was designed by Duncan Macleod of the Bengal Engineers and was built in Italianate style between 1829 and 1837. Thomas also visited Greece and Egypt and there is even evidence from the titles of his paintings that he visited places in what are now Iraq and Iran.

Did Thomas make a journey to the East in order to thwart his creditors? There are good grounds for believing that sometime at the beginning of the 1840s he had made a journey to India and on the way visited Greece and Egypt. This journey cannot be corroborated, but in later life Thomas spoke of travels to all of these countries. In 1847, for example, soon after he had arrived in St Petersburg, he visited the home of Charlotte Bourne, who was working for a noble Russian family and who on her return to England wrote *Russian Chit-Chat*, which was published anonymously in 1856. She records meeting Thomas several times in St Petersburg and gives some clues to his previous travels:

> "*March 6th, 1847: Mr A, the English painter, to dinner: a talented man; has seen India and Egypt; taken views on the Ganges and the Nile. The Indian idol temples much more splendid than the Mahometan ones. Moscow reminds him of a Mahometan town with its many domes. Delhi a fine old town, the ruins are six miles in length. The English society, at St Petersburg, divided into cliques – he preferred the Russian.*"
>
> "*March 9th: Mr A. has sketched in Egypt with the thermometer at 120F; the sky there often red. Tried to compare Eothen and Titmarsh: I think the first is the*

most clever and amusing, but the most egotistical; the second like an imitation of it, (or it might be that I read the second in a small edition;) there is a want of looking at things seriously in both, which is the defect of many books of the present day, thought there are at times very nice feelings expressed, particularly in the latter. I think the milk of the intellectual existence of each tells much, – in the first Homer, in the second the Arabian Nights."

> "*March 12th: Mr A-son again: he says the remains of Grecian architecture sink into utter insignificance by the side of those of the Egyptians and the Indians; these two appear to have been formed about the same time; they bear marks of resemblance without seeming to have been taken the one from the other. In the caves of Ellora are obelisks raised, evidently for the same purpose as those in Egypt – the making of astronomical observations. The architecture of the middle ages is more perfect than that of Greece and Rome. The first impression, on approaching the Pyramids, is one of disappointment; the mind cannot take in their immensity.*"

> "*At Pultowa the climate is so mild that people sit now with open windows. A, E and M-orf to dinner; asked the first whether the character Eothen derives of the Arabs is true? He said he had not found it so. The Greeks a very degraded race, no dependence to be placed on them, but the Turks are a fine nation, and what they have once promised they never fail to perform. He had visited Lord Byron, at Newstead; his lordship was often very amiable and agreeable, at other times violent. He brought with him a design for a magnificent Cathedral, to be erected at Manchester.*"[7]

Also, amongst Thomas Atkinson's papers preserved in the Dahlquist Collection are lists of paintings in his possession or for sale. One document, for example, compiled in 1856 in Russia, lists the following paintings that are offered as surety for a loan:

Indian Antiquities
Greek Antiquities
Banks of River Jumti
Ruined Masjid Jounpur
Night scene Abyssinia

Temple of Kurkotuc nag. India
Temple of the Sun, Palmyra
Tombs of Kutgurks
Compo.Indian architecture
Sarai and bridge, India
Jumna Masjid
Great Sphinx
Temple of Carnac
Memnon
El uxor
Ramesion Thebes

Banks of Gumti
Tomb of Cyrus
15 views in Sicily and India

Together with other paintings of scenes in Italy, this list of paintings indicates that Thomas travelled extensively in Greece, Egypt, present-day Syria, Abyssinia and Iran during what was likely a journey to India and back, probably in the early 1840s. To date, no other evidence has been found to substantiate these travels, other than the pictures, which do not appear to be copies of other works.   ■

1. Memoirs of Anna Maria Wilhelmina Pickering, Hodder and Stoughton, London, 1903, pp42-43
2. In August 2015 the importance of Atkinson's work was recognised with a specially commissioned plaque on the wall within the chapel.
3. Gothic Ornaments selected from the different Cathedrals and Churches of England, By TW Atkinson, architect, London, published by the author, 8 Upper Stamford St, 1829.
4. The Builder, 31 August 1861.
5. The drawings of the Hazarduari Palace were sold in 1979 at Christie's auction house, London.

6. It is not clear if or when Thomas visited Newstead Abbey to meet Lord Byron. In 1818 – when Thomas was only 19 – Byron sold the Abbey to Colonel Thomas Wildman for £92,000. Wildman was known to the Spencer Stanhope and Lady Elizabeth Spencer Stanhope writes of visiting there, so perhaps Thomas visited the house after it had been sold.
7. Russian Chit Chat; or sketches of a residence in Russia, By a lady, Ed. by her sister, Longman, Brown, Green, Longmans and Roberts, London, 1856 Charlotte was employed by Senator Iurii Alekseevich Dolgoruki and his wife Elizaveta Dolgorukaia.

A boss from Lincoln Cathedral

Chapter
THREE

ARRIVAL IN ST PETERSBURG

Although we don't know exactly when Thomas made his journey to the Middle East and India prior to arriving in St Petersburg in 1846, we do know that he left England for Hamburg in 1842. Among the papers preserved by the Atkinson family is a passport issued to Thomas by the Free Hanseatic Republics of Lubeck, Bremen and Hamburg. This large, imposing document, issued in London on 4 July 1842, states "*By the Agent and Consul General for the Free Hanseatic Republics of Lubeck, Bremen and Hamburgh, resident in Great Britain, These are to request and require all those whom it may concern, to allow Mr Thomas Witlam Atkinson, national of Great Britain, a Gentleman going to Hamburgh, to pass freely without let or hindrance and to afford him all aid and assistance.*"[1] The passport also carries a second stamp showing that on 13 July in the same year he was given a visa that allowed him to travel on to Berlin.

The description 'Gentleman' on this Hanseatic passport would have meant a great deal to Thomas. Having come from a humble background, he had risen from a lowly stone cutter to society architect. Now, despite his recent financial woes, he could still be described in a way that was in itself almost a guarantee of good treatment and a reception in even the grandest houses.

The immediate reason for Thomas' journey to Hamburg was the devastating fire in 1842 that destroyed most of the city, particularly St Nicholas Church – the *Nikolaikirche*. Thomas probably thought that there were good employment prospects in helping to reconstruct the city. The city fathers quickly decided to build a new church on the old site and organised an architectural competition to decide upon a new design. It was won by the architect Gottfried Semper with a classical Roman

St Nicholas Church, Hamburg

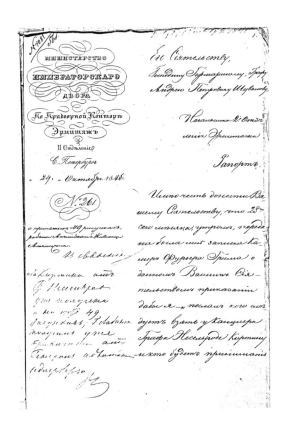

Russian officials discuss Thomas Atkinson's paintings

domed structure. However, despite winning the competition, Semper's design was not popular with the town's citizens as it did not fit into the city's townscape and was not in the Gothic revival style that was growing in popularity in Germany.

The whole issue went back to the adjudication committee, who decided that the English architect George Gilbert Scott[2] (1811-1878) – who had come third in the original competition – should get the contract. Despite his youth, Scott already had extensive experience in the restoration of medieval churches and was a strong advocate of the Gothic revival style. He proposed a massive, 86 metre-long nave, with a 28 metre-high vault, strongly influenced by French and English Gothic styles, although with a typically German pointed spire.[3]

Construction started in 1846, and on 27 September 1863 the church was consecrated. The 147.3 metre-high spire was finished in 1874, thus making the Church of St Nicholas the highest building in the world until the completion of Rouen cathedral in 1876. The extent to which Thomas was involved in the church or in designing other buildings in Hamburg remains to be discovered, although the city's destruction in the Second World War means it is very unlikely that any of his work survives there. According to his entry in the *Dictionary of National Biography*, Thomas entered the competition for the church, but was not successful. This would not have stopped him working on aspects of the designs for Scott, or even on other reconstruction projects. Either way, he had left the city by the time building work actually started on the church.

The Builder, in its obituary of Thomas, says that even though he did not win the Hamburg competition, "*he made some progress in a work illustrative of his church at Cheetham Hill, which was announced by London publishers; but, if regularly*

Beloselsky-Belozersky Palace and Anichkov Bridge, St Petersburg

published, it does not seem to have got into circulation."[4] What this building was remains unknown, although in Russia he mentioned to one diarist a design he had made for a large cathedral in Manchester.

One important mystery remains concerning Thomas' stay in Hamburg. In the *Manchester Courier and Lancashire General Advertiser* for 11 April 1846 there is a small obituary:

> "*On the 3rd inst., at Hamburg, in his 23rd year, after a long illness of near four years, John William, eldest son of Mr T. W. Atkinson, architect, formerly of this town. His talents were various: as a marine painter they would have been great, as shewn by his sketches, one of which, the 'Phantom Ships', is of a very high order.*"

Thus we have it that Thomas' only son by his first marriage to

Rebecca Mercer died in Hamburg. He was buried three days after his death at the English Episcopal Church in the city. If he had been ill for four years, his illness would have started in 1842, the year that Thomas travelled to Hamburg. Did he take John with him? The fact that the report refers to Thomas being "formerly of this town" (ie Manchester), certainly indicates that he had settled in Hamburg and explains the decision to bury his son there.

There is no evidence that Thomas returned to England from Hamburg during the early 1840s. We are left to ponder on his state of mind during this period. He had left England under a financial cloud, his business reputation in tatters. Hamburg at least offered him the chance to work as a jobbing architect, where he would not need access to credit. His son, suffering from a serious illness, has joined him but has died, aged only 22. So in only a few years Thomas appears to have lost his

John Fane, 6th Earl of Westmorland

business, his wife and daughters and, tragically, his son. We can only speculate on his state of mind, but his decision to go to Russia, at the same time abandoning his profession and taking the decision to travel to some of the most remote and dangerous places on Earth seem to suggest a desire to get away from the pressures of the world. Perhaps it explains his detached attitude to danger, set out in the introduction to *Oriental and Western Siberia*:

> *"Mine is a simple narrative of facts, taken from journals kept with scrupulous care during the whole journey, often under the influence of great fatigue and amid the pressure of numerous difficulties. I suffered much both from hunger and thirst, have run many risks and on several occasions have been placed in most critical situations with the tribes of Central Asia – more particularly when among the convicts escaped from the Chinese penal settlements – desperate characters who hold the lives of men cheap. I have several times looked upon what appeared inevitable death, and have had a fair allowance of hair-breadth escapes when riding and sketching on the brinks of precipices with a perpendicular depth of 1500 feet below me."[5]*

Others would have regarded his plan for travel in such remote areas as foolhardy in the extreme. If the 'tribes of Central Asia' didn't get him, the climatic extremes of deserts and snowstorms certainly would.

From Hamburg Thomas must have made his way to Berlin, then the capital of Prussia. His Hanseatic passport carried a visa that was also valid for travel to Berlin. One source at least states he travelled in order to find more work, not because of any decision connected to the death of his son. In her memoirs, Anna Maria Pickering says that Thomas decided to travel to Russia a result of a meeting with Tsar Nicholas 1:

> *"On the Emperor of Russia passing through the city, he was so struck with his work that he sent for the architect, and at once engaged him to go to St Petersburg. He was employed for many years on Imperial works, both in St Petersburg and in other parts of the Russian empire, including Siberia."[6]*

This comment is slightly curious in that Thomas is not known to have built anything during the years he lived in Russia. However, it is quite possible that the story of him meeting

the Tsar is true. There were also other reasons that drew him towards Russia, and to Siberia in particular, not least his meeting in Berlin with the great German geographer and scientist Alexander von Humboldt, who had himself, in the late 1820s, travelled through the Urals and the Altai Mountains of Western Siberia. In a letter written from St Petersburg in 1854, Thomas reminded the great man of their first encounter: "Sir, In 1846 you very kindly gave me a letter of introduction to Admiral Lutke[7]…" The *Dictionary of National Biography* entry for Thomas suggests that Humboldt was a major inspiration to Thomas. It states: "Inspired by Alexander von Humboldt's accounts of Siberia, Atkinson then moved to St Petersburg, after a short stay in Berlin. There, in 1846, he abandoned architecture as a profession for the pursuits of an explorer and topographical artist."[8]

Thomas also received some support and encouragement from John Fane, the 11th Earl of Westmorland and, from 1841-1851, minister plenipotentiary at Berlin. Fane wrote a letter of recommendation to Andrew Buchanan[9], *Chargé d'Affaires* at the British Legation in St Petersburg. It is likely that Thomas met Humboldt himself through the Fanes, as the latter is known to have been a friend of the Earl and his wife Priscilla. Humboldt was just the sort of man that Thomas would look up to, a self-taught renaissance man, a household name in his lifetime and also a talented artist.

Exactly when he arrived in St Petersburg is not known, although it must have been some time after his son died in Hamburg on 3rd April. The best clue comes from a letter Andrew Buchanan sent back from St Petersburg in the diplomatic pouch to Lord Palmerston, the newly appointed Foreign Secretary in London. Dated from the end of October 1846, it says that Thomas had asked Buchanan to make representations to Count Nesselrode[10], the Foreign Minister, "some time ago", suggesting at least a month or two previously.

In *Oriental and Western Siberia*, Thomas recalls the course of events:

> *"After due consideration I determined to apply to the Emperor for especial permission to travel and sketch, feeling certain that if this were granted, there would be no difficulties: if refused, I would not make the attempt. I wrote a letter, which was most kindly laid before His Imperial Majesty by Mr Buchanan, Charge d'Affaires; and*

in three days received an answer from Count Nesselrode, informing me that the Emperor had granted my request, and that orders had been issued to the Minister of the Interior and other authorities to prepare for me all the necessary papers.[11]"

As previously noted, Buchanan noted Thomas' arrival in St Petersburg and reported back to Lord Palmerston that he had suggested the artist might like to pass on any useful information he came across in his travels.

Buchanan had not missed the fact that the Russians had offered Thomas unprecedented access to travel in parts of the Russian empire that few British travellers had ever visited. *"Every facility"*, as set out in the special passport, meant that Thomas would have the same rights to horses, carriages, provisions, guides and Cossack protection, as an imperial officer. He intended to use his newly-issued passport to travel right across the continent, as far as the Chinese border.

Count Nesselrode's reply to Andrew Buchanan still survives amongst the Atkinson family papers[12]. Written in August 1846, it asks Buchanan to tell Thomas about the decision. A second letter from Nesselrode to Buchanan, dated 19 September 1846, notes that Thomas had offered some of his paintings from his travels in India, Greece and Egypt to the Tsar, who graciously declined to accept them. Undeterred, Thomas was now in possession of a passport that would allow him to travel unimpeded across Russia.

This was a privilege indeed. I cannot find another example of such a passport being granted. Other travellers took their chances on the post roads through Siberia, waiting for hours, sometimes days, for horses to be found and giving way if an official was travelling the same route. It is the first of many examples of Thomas making an impression and perhaps winning favours that would be denied another person. So often he got the best out of someone, whether it be the Cossack officers he met while travelling, the Decembrist exiles he met in Siberia, the governors of mines or of entire regions. Many of them went out of their way to help him and this stands as a tribute to the character of a man whom we can only know from the faint echoes of the impact he had on other people that still resonate to this day.

The extent to which Thomas came to depend on this little

scrap of Imperial paper can be gauged from those comments in *Oriental and Western Siberia* mentioned in Chapter One:

> *"I am deeply indebted to the late Emperor of Russia,"* he wrote, *"for without his passport I should have been stopped at every government and insurmountable difficulties would have been thrown in my way. This slip of paper proved a talisman wherever presented in his dominions and swept down every obstacle raised to bar my progress.[13]"*

Buchanan must have realised that information gleaned by Thomas on his travels would be of enormous interest to his colleagues in Whitehall. Although not declared enemies at this point, within eight years Great Britain and Imperial Russia would be at war in the Crimea. Already tensions were growing between the two great powers as they struggled over the carcass of the decaying Ottoman Empire and how to fill the power vacuum left in Europe by the defeat of Napoleon. Nor was Britain a disinterested observer of Russia's Far Eastern southern neighbour, China. Only four years before, in August 1842, Britain had imposed the unequal Treaty of Nanking on the Qing rulers of China, forcing them to open their ports to foreign trade and to accept British-supplied opium. That was followed in 1844 by the Treaty of Whampoa that imposed similar conditions on behalf of France. Before long both countries would land troops in China and occupy the capital. The world was opening up for trade and the prospect of transporting Chinese goods to Europe overland was, for the first time, being considered. As Eastern and Far Eastern trade began to open up, so strategic considerations began to grow, not least in relation to India. Soon this preoccupation over who controlled what in Central Asia and its hinterlands would become known as 'The Great Game' and would occupy the minds of politicians and diplomats in Europe for the next 70 years. Without realising it, Thomas was about to traverse some of the very lands that were at the heart of this often mystifying, but always engrossing, diplomatic duel.

Although he had been issued with an unusual passport, Thomas was not the first European to travel in Siberia. By the 1840s there was no lack of travellers who had reached the Urals and then moved eastwards to Barnaul and the northern foothills of the Altai Mountain range in southern Siberia and from there on to Irkutsk and Lake Baikal. In 1840 the English magistrate Charles Cottrell had travelled from

Moscow to Irkutsk and even as far as Nerchinsk, stating in his book *Recollections of Siberia*[14] that it was a journey *"which we believe no other living Englishman has made, except two missionaries many years established in Selenginsk."* Other travellers included the Irishman Peter Dobell[15] and the remarkable Captain John Dundas Cochrane[16], who between 1820-1824 had walked from Europe to Kamchatka on the Pacific Ocean and back again. Even the remarkable blind traveller, James Holman, had reached Irkutsk in 1822, travelling alone and with only limited mobility. There he was suspected of being a spy and was seized by the secret police and deported to Poland. On his return to London he published an account of his travels[17].

In 1840 and 1841 the great British geographer Roderick Murchison had been involved in two scientific expeditions to remote parts of Russia, including the far north and also the Urals and Altai Mountains. Both trips had received support from Tsar Nicholas I. Murchison's findings and detailed maps had been published in 1845, as *The Geology of Russia*[18]. In fact, it is quite possible that Thomas had read a copy of Murchison's book, as he visited many of the same places described by the latter, and in the same order. And even one of Thomas' illustrations for *Oriental and Western Siberia* bears a remarkable similarity to a drawing that appears in Murchison's book.

Humboldt had also travelled in roughly the same areas in 1829 and his descriptions had no doubt enthused Thomas, particularly his descriptions of the Kazakh Steppes[19]. In an attempt to understand the volcanic activity that had shaped Central Asia, Humboldt had travelled to Barnaul in the Altai before heading south to Riddersk, Zyrianovsky, Ust Kamenogorsk (modern-day Oskemen) and then to Lake Zaisan on the frontier of Chinese Dzungaria, before returning to Orenburg.

The ambition of Thomas' proposed route caught the attention of Buchanan, who very explicitly suggested "several points of political and commercial interest" about which Thomas might like to tell Her Majesty's Government when he was next in town. Was it spying? Not in anything but the loosest sense. Thomas intended to travel in open view of the authorities, often in company with Cossack guards or state officials. A trained spy might be able to make assessments of transportation movements or to know the regimental badge

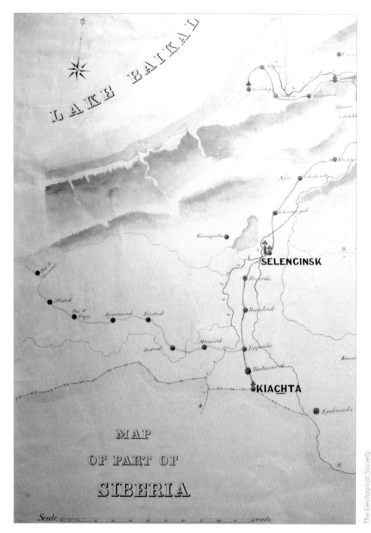

Part of Charles Austin's massive map of the Trans-Baikal region

General Mikhail Nikolaevich Muravyev-Vilensky, who
employed Lucy Finley as a governess for his daugter.

of every soldier he passed on the road, but Buchanan's pitch to Thomas was more akin to a call on his sense of nationalism, a typical request to pass on anything he thought might be of interest. As it turned out, he got more than he bargained for.

There was one other little mystery associated with Thomas' passport. It concerns the identity of the *"Englishman who has been for some time residing in this country"* who was mentioned in Buchanan message as the person who would accompany Thomas on his journey. That turns out to have been Charles Edward Austin (1819-1893). Austin, who came from Gloucestershire, was 20 years younger than Thomas and had trained as a railway engineer on the Great Western Railway, for whom he worked until the early 1840s. He subsequently moved to St Petersburg where he worked on steam navigation on the Volga, publishing a treatise on the then state of the river traffic and its management.

The trip he started with Thomas was the first of two tours he made into Siberia. During the second, on which he was accompanied by his wife, he visited some of the exile stations of Siberia, as well as the mines at Nerchinsk, and the Sayan Mountains along the Chinese frontier. Like the Atkinsons, he resided for some time at Irkutsk, although during his first trip he got into trouble with the authorities when his actions were seen as suspicious by none other than the Governor of Eastern Siberia, General Nikolai Muravyev-Amursky, a man who was later to play a significant role in the Atkinson saga. One source describes the incident thus:

"At the end of 1848, Muravyev was on an inspection trip through the gubernias of Eniseisk and Irkutsk, devoting the majority of his time to the Transbaikal, and was gathering data needed to support a proposal that he visit Kamchatka, where no other governor of Siberia had ever been. While on his way back from Tsurukhaita, on the line of Cossack stations through Kiakhta to Verkhneudinsk, he learned that an Englishman named Austin, ostensibly pursuing geological investigations, had crossed Lake Baikal and proceeded by way of Verkhneudinsk and Chita to Nerchinsk. There he had arranged to have a large raft built on which he planned to sail down the Shilka and the Amur to the mouth of that river, hoping to find a whaler or other vessel on which he could cross the Pacific, or which would take him straight to Europe.

Muravyev was highly suspicious of foreigners in his area, particularly of Englishmen, and, convinced that Austin was a spy, ordered one of his officers back to Nerchinsk to catch up with Austin and to bring him back to Irkutsk, "dead or alive". The officer brought Austin back to Irkutsk within ten days. Muravyev immediately reported on this incident to St Petersburg, and in a personal letter to Perovsky, he held forth on the jeopardy in which the project of occupying the Amur was placed by uninvited guests who were spying for the English government. Muravyev seems to have been obsessed with the idea that the British might suddenly seize Sakhalin, or the mouth of the Amur, an idea to which he clung for years. Muravyev's fears, it is true, were shared by others. Thus, Perovsky, in his reply wrote: "It is not without foundation that you consider it necessary to warn the English, and that the time has come when this should not be postponed. I fully share your view, but Count Nesselrode is not thinking along these lines." [20]

It is not explicit, but it seems that Muravyev could not deport Austin, as he had wished. Austin continued to work in Russia and later worked in Turkey and in South America. By the time that Austin was arrested, he and Thomas had long since separated for reasons that will soon become apparent. But until the end of 1847 – Thomas' first year of travel – they were together as travelling partners and he is frequently mentioned in Thomas' travel diary for 1847. Austin's obituary records that he was a good linguist, which could explain Thomas' decision to travel with him[21]. In 1862 Austin presented to the Geological Society of London, of which he was a Fellow, some notes on his Siberian explorations. Sadly, these can no longer be located, although the Society still holds a series of remarkable large-scale maps, drawn and coloured by Austin, of the area between Irkutsk and Nerchinsk in Eastern Siberia.

Thomas says that one of the first people he consulted about his proposed journey through Siberia was Admiral Peter Ivanovich Ricord[22] (1776-1855), one of the founding members of the Russian Geographical Society and commanding officer of the Kamchatka Peninsula from 1817-1822, where he introduced the cultivation of potatoes. Ricord was Italian by birth but spoke perfect English, having served as a midshipman in the Royal Navy under Nelson. He had only ever travelled across Siberia on the Great Post Road, which

Admiral Pyotr Ivanovich Ricord

passes to the north of the Altai region, but knew a great deal about the regions bordering the Pacific Ocean and the Sea of Okhotsk. Thus Thomas lost no time once he was in St Petersburg in seeking out information that would be useful to him on his journey to the East.

In those first few days and weeks in St Petersburg, Thomas was already trying to make connections and to find out information about what he could expect to encounter on his travels. He may have fallen in with Austin because the geologist/engineer had lived in the country for several years and probably spoke Russian.

He was soon working his contact list, particularly those prominent geographers recommended to him by Humboldt. We don't know how he met Lucy Sherrard Finley, the 29-year-old Englishwoman he was later to marry. The fact that she was working in St Petersburg as a governess to the daughter of a Russian general, who also happened to be president of the Russian Geographical Society, may explain the encounter. Did Thomas meet her when he called upon General Mikhail Nikolaievich Muravyev-Vilensky?[23] Quite possibly. However the meeting occurred, it was to have a massive impact on the lives of both Thomas and Lucy.

Born in 1817 in Sunderland, County Durham, to Matthew and Mary Ann Finley, Lucy was the fourth child and eldest daughter of ten children. Her father was a schoolteacher but he had probably started his career as a mariner. His father and grandfather, both called Robert Finley, had been master mariners. Lucy's grandfather Robert (1707-1806) was mainly involved in carrying coal from the coal-mining and ship-building centre of Monkwearmouth on the north bank of the Wear River in Sunderland, to London. He was also involved in the cross-Channel trade bringing French wines to the British market and he also made at least one trip to St Petersburg carrying hemp. It seems likely, therefore, that Lucy had heard tales of the frozen north throughout her life.

Lucy's mother Mary Ann was born in Stepney in London's East End and she and Matthew were married at St Dunstan's in the East on 25 April 1810. Just north of the expanding docks of the Port of London, the area had long been associated with maritime trade and it is reasonable to suspect that the Matthew had first visited Stepney and met Mary Ann whilst on a voyage down from Monkwearmouth.

Matthew and Mary Ann moved to the north in 1813 where four of their children, including Lucy, were born, but they returned to Stepney at some point between 1824 and 1826. The move may well have had something to do with finances for there is evidence that in 1831, when Lucy was 14, Matthew Finley was an insolvent debtor.

Before she went to Russia, Lucy had set up a toy business at the family home at 4 Waterloo Terrace (now 518-554 Commercial Road). Records show that as late as 1846 the venture was in Lucy's name, even though by this time she had been in Russia for six years. By 1848 it was being held in her mother's name. Most likely Mary Ann had kept the business in Lucy's name thinking that she would return, but when that seemed unlikely after her marriage to Thomas, had transferred it to her own name. It should be pointed out that 'toy' in this context may not necessarily mean what it does today. In the first half of the nineteenth century, a toy would generally mean what today we would call a knick-knack or ornament.

In St Petersburg Lucy was one of many young Englishwomen who arrived to take up positions as governesses to the children of Russia's leading families. Her charge was Sophie, the only daughter of General Mikhail Nikolaevich Muravyev-Vilensky. Lucy would have been provided with a good wage and accommodation and would have had a status well above that of a house servant. With good fortune, she could save enough to provide her with an annuity in later life and perhaps, if she was lucky, she would meet a man and make an advantageous marriage.

We have already noted that Thomas was doing the social rounds in St Petersburg and was recorded by Charlotte Bourne as a visitor to her house on at least three occasions early in 1847[24]. At some point a spark of romance seems to have been kindled between him and the unattached Lucy. Although nearly 20 years her senior, he would have appeared to her as a man of action, someone about to embark on a fabulously romantic journey, painting the wildernesses of Siberia and dealing with the ferocious tribesmen of the steppes.

But in the immediate future nothing was to pass between the two. Thomas continued to make his preparations to leave and Lucy continued teaching her pupil the rudiments of French,

English and Arithmetic. Before finally leaving for the East Thomas made contact with yet another source, this time a mining engineer introduced to him by the Minister of Finance, who had previously worked in the Altai. "*From him I collected much valuable information relative to my route,*" says Thomas[25].

Early in March 1847 he set off for Moscow on the first leg of his journey, where he stayed for a few weeks. There he took part in the great festival to commemorate the 700th anniversary of the city:

> "*During the evening a tableau was given representing the four elements, Air Earth, Fire, and Water, which were personated by four beautiful young ladies, whose appearance called forth immense applause. Without dropping the curtain, this picture was changed by suddenly drawing off the dresses; which was done by someone beneath the stage. One young lady (whether of earth or heaven seemed difficult to determine) was kneeling on one knee on a piece of rock, and when the signal was given, was jerked from her place and turned feet upwards on the floor – a position for which she was evidently not prepared. Many of the spectators began to laugh, but this was very properly hushed by His Imperial Majesty in an instant; in the next, the lady was divested of her first costume and again took her place on the rock, with the additional charm of a deep blush spreading over her face.*"[26]

Thomas also met with 'Professor Fischer', whom he had met previously. This was probably the German-born Dr Sebastian Fischer, who until 1841 was head of the central military hospital at Qasr-el-Aini in Egypt and who was an expert on crustacea. It is possible that this is where Thomas met him. In 1843 Fischer had moved to St Petersburg, but also had connections to Moscow. He was a friend of Alexander von Middendorf (1815-1894), a Baltic German zoologist and explorer, who between 1843-45 had travelled to the Taymyr Peninsula in northern Siberia and then along the coast of the Sea of Okhotsk, before entering the lower Amur River valley in the Russian Far East. Thomas had also met Middendorf, at dinner in St Petersburg at the house of Charlotte Bourne. Fischer put Thomas in touch with Dr Friedrich August von Gebler (1782-1850), inspector of hospitals in the Altai region, with whom Thomas later spent many evenings in Barnaul. We will come back to him later.

After 15 days in Moscow, Thomas was off again, leaving on the 5th March for Ekaterinburg and the east. It would be almost a year before he returned to Moscow. And then it was only for the few days it took to renew his acquaintance with Lucy – and to marry her. ∎

1. Document in the possession of Paul Dahlquist, Atkinson's great-grandson. The three Hanseatic city-states remained independent until 1867, when they joined the North German League. Three years later they became part of the newly formed German state.

2. Scott was the leading architect of the Gothic revival, responsible for more than 800 buildings, including the Albert Memorial, the Midland Hotel at St Pancras and the Foreign and Commonwealth Office. See http://www.vam.ac.uk/content/articles/s/sir-george-gilbert-scott/

3. On 28 July 1943 the church was heavily damaged by Allied bombing during extensive air raids on Hamburg. The roof collapsed and the interior of the nave suffered heavy damage. The basic structure of the gothic church remained intact to a large extent and reconstruction was a realistic option. Nevertheless, it was decided to demolish the nave while leaving the spire untouched. In 1951 the nave was finally demolished and the rubble was partially used for the reinforcement of the banks of the river Elbe. The remaining spire is now a memorial to the victims of World War Two.

4. *The Builder*, op cit.

5. OWS, op.cit, p.vi.

6. Pickering, op.cit, pp42-3.

7. Count Fyodor Petrovich Litke (1797-1882) was a Baltic German navigator, Arctic explorer, geographer and member of the Russian Academy of Science in St Petersburg. He was tutor to Tsar Nicholas I's second son Constantine and president of the Russian Geographical Society 1845-50.

8. DNB

9. See https://en.wikipedia.org/wiki/Sir_Andrew_Buchanan,_1st_Baronet

10. https://en.wikipedia.org/wiki/Karl_Nesselrode

11. Thomas Witlam Atkinson, *Oriental and Western Siberia*, 1858, Hurst and Blackett, London, p1-2.

12. See Dahlquist Papers

13. Ibid, pvii.

14. Charles Herbert Cottrell, *Recollections of Siberia in the years 1840 and 1841*, John W Parker, London, 1842.

15. Peter Dobell, *Travels in Kamchatka and Siberia, with a narrative of a residence in China*, London, 1830 (2 vols).

16. See John Dundas Cochrane, *Narrative of a Pedestrian Journey through Russia and Siberian Tartary, to the Frontiers of China to the Frozen Sea and Kamtchatka*, London, 1824 (2 vols).

17. James Holman, *Travels Through Russia, Siberia, Poland, Austria, Saxony, Prussia, Hanover, & C. & C: Undertaken During the Years 1822, 1823 and 1824, While Suffering from Total Blindness, and Comprising an Account of the Author Being Conducted a State Prisoner from the Eastern Parts of Siberia*, Smith, Elder and Co, London, 1825.

18. Roderick Impey Murchison, *The Geology of Russia in Europe and the Ural Mountains*, John Murray, London 1845.

19. For a summary of Humboldt's writings on Central Asia see W Macgillivray, *The Life, Travels and Researches of Baron Humboldt*, T Nelson and Son, London, 1860, pp348ff.

20. MA Thesis, Eric E. Oulashin, *Nicholas N Muraviev, Conqueror of the Black Dragon*, Portland State University, 1971, http://pdxscholar.library.pdx.edu/open_access_etds/1465/

21. Austin's obituary can be found in the *Proceedings of the Institution of Civil Engineers* http://www.icevirtuallibrary.com/content/article/10.1680/imotp.1893.20450

22. Thomas spells his name Rickardt.

23. Muravyev-Vilensky was an important figure in mid-nineteenth century Russia, scion of a famous family, many of whom had supported the unsuccessful Decembrist Revolt in 1825. Lucy's connections within the family were to serve her and Thomas very well during their travels.

24. *Russian Chit-Chat*, op cit.

25. OWS, op cit, p2.

26. Ibid, p3.

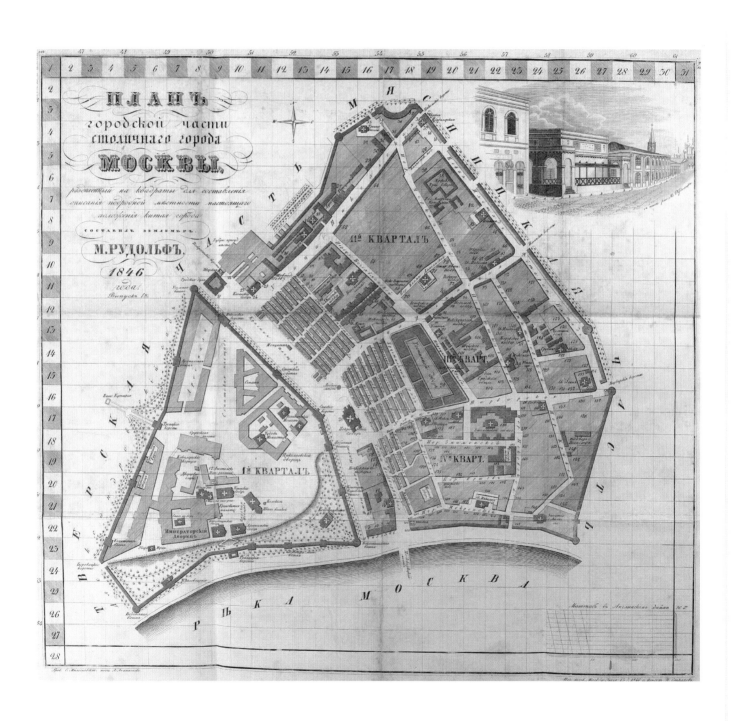

Map of Moscow in 1846

Chapter
FOUR

1847: THOMAS' SOLO JOURNEY TO THE URALS, THE ALTAI AND THE NORTHERN KAZAKH STEPPES

Together with his travelling companion, Charles Austin, Thomas left Moscow on 5th March, just as the first tentative signs of spring were appearing, setting out for Yekaterinburg 1,400 kilometres to the east on the other side of the Urals in a type of large sledge called a *vashock*, pulled by four horses. Progress was quick on the ice roads, even though winter was coming to an end and the ice was beginning to break up. The next day he passed through Vladimir, with its five-domed cathedral, 200 kilometres east of Moscow and by the following morning was in Nijni Novgorod, where he visited the governor, who bought him breakfast. In those days Nijni Novgorod was the venue for the great Makaryev Trade Fair, held every autumn for six weeks, which attracted millions of visitors from all over Russia and Asia. After an extra day in the town, Thomas pushed on to Kazan, arriving just after five in the morning on the 11th March and surviving a serious crash on the way in which everything was thrown out of the sledge.

Lying at the confluence of the Volga and Kazanka rivers, today Kazan is the capital of the Tartarstan Republic. Here he was received by the governor, General Irakly Abromovich Baratinsky and his wife, who introduced him to various professors at the university. But with the threat of warm weather and the break-up of the ice roads imminent, Thomas wasted no time and once again, after a day, pushed on towards Perm.

Soon Thomas was approaching the Urals, which he was anxious to see. But even at the best of times the Urals are hardly an imposing mountain chain. The mountains on this route rise gently and barely stand out against the landscape. He arrived in Perm on the 15th and left two days later for Yekaterinburg in drenching rain. Two extra horses were attached to the *vashock* to pull it through the slushy ice. At Kungur two men attempted to steal Thomas's deerhound. He tells how he followed them into a yard, where he pulled out

his pistol and persuaded them to let the dog out of a shed into which they had locked it. "*There are several stations along this part of the road notoriously bad, demanding unceasing vigilance from the traveller,*" he wrote. It would not be the last time he had to draw a weapon. At 10pm on the 18th he arrived in Yekaterinburg, having crossed the important psychological boundary from Europe into Asia earlier in the day.

In Yekaterinburg Thomas presented his letter of introduction from the Minister of Finance to the chief of the Urals, who received him well and placed him under the care of a fellow Englishman, who had been in Russian service for the previous decade. "*I felt at home, being able to talk in my own tongue*", writes Thomas. He was to stay for a month. It was coming towards the end of the Lent fast and Easter, a significant religious festival in Orthodox Russia, was only a week away. Thomas was invited to stay and witness the 'ceremony of kissing' and he made use of his time there to collect more information about places he could expect to see on his route.

Over the next few weeks Thomas took the opportunity to explore the Urals, and in particular the many mines and metalworks in the region. Here he was following closely in the footsteps of both Roderick Murchison and Alexander von Humboldt. As a former stonemason he would have been interested in the fascinating rock formations and rare minerals in the region. And in the homes of the mine officials scattered across the Urals and into the Altai he could be sure of finding a good welcome and ample signs of civilisation.

A note of caution about Thomas' itinerary should be mentioned here. Neither of Thomas' two books on his travels contain either a detailed itinerary connected to dates, nor a strictly sequential ordering of the text. This is a serious problem and has been the subject of much speculation. Some reviewers said they were unable to follow his routes, while others suggested he had fabricated parts of his journeys. In later years even a charge of plagiarism was brought against Thomas. We will return to some of these issues, but for now, the inconsistencies and omissions of his text can best be explained by his marriage to Lucy. This had two consequences: first, he decided to return from the Altai to Russia in February 1848 to marry her and this meant that part

Watercolour of a cavern on the Chusowaya River

in the Urals by Thomas Atkinson

of the journey – through the Urals, the Altai and part of what is now northern Kazakhstan – had, of necessity, to be repeated. Thomas chose not to explain this to his readers and therefore his account of this part of the journey contains material from both of these visits to the region, although it mostly follows his 1847 visit.

Second, and far more significant, was the fact that Thomas told Lucy when he married her that he was a widower. This was untrue, as when he married Lucy in February 1848, Rebecca, his first wife, was still very much alive and living in Chelsea, London. We don't know the circumstances of the split with Rebecca, as neither of them has left an account of how the marriage ended. Tentatively, we can date it to some point at the beginning of the 1840s. If so, there is a reasonable chance that it was connected to the fallout from his bankruptcy. His decision to travel to the East, to go and work in Germany and then his decision to travel to Russia with the clear intention of staying away for several years all suggest that he had no intention of returning to his first wife in England. That said, it needs to be explained why he did not tell the truth to Lucy. Clearly he could not ask her to travel with him without being married. Even in far-off Russia, it would not have been acceptable to travel with a woman to whom he was not married. And if he had told her he was already married, that would have been an end of it; divorce was almost unheard of and he was unlikely to have travelled back to England to obtain one, even if it was possible.

That left Thomas with little option but to tell Lucy that he was a widower and hope that no-one questioned him too closely. Ultimately, it was a foolish decision, but Thomas may well have thought he had little alternative. At this time, bigamy was still a very serious offence under British law, which could have resulted in a prison sentence for Thomas, even though his second marriage had taken place abroad. That may be sufficient to explain his decision to cover up his first marriage completely and write up his travels as if he was travelling alone. As far as we know, Lucy only found out about the existence of his first wife after Thomas died in 1861, when Rebecca came forward to claim his estate. The more one thinks about this, the odder it seems, not least because Lucy was to give birth to a child during their first year travelling together. Hiding this from his readers – and his former wife – was an audacious thing to attempt, but it also had major consequences for the narrative of his books. He could mention none of the remarkable events that involved Lucy or his child during the

A view on the Chusowaya River

in the Urals by Thomas Atkinson

Tagilsk by Thomas Atkinson

course of almost six years travelling together. This fateful decision was to determine the outcome of many subsequent events, even possibly his decision to stay away from England for so many years.

However, all is not as it seems. Despite the confusion in Thomas' published books, he kept a very detailed account of his travels in the diaries he wrote during the journeys. These five diaries, now held in the archives of the Royal Geographical Society, make explicit his deep affection for Lucy and show how much he valued her contribution to their adventure. After all, she was a fluent Russian speaker and took full charge of handling relations with the Cossack guards and Kalmuck guides with whom the couple travelled. She it was who negotiated with the post-house officials to obtain fresh horses and provisions and provided the introduction to countless officials and exiled aristocrats that she knew of because of her connections to the Muravyev family. Without

her, Thomas would have been lost and he was well aware of that fact.

Unaware of the circumstances behind his decision to exclude Lucy from the narrative, some commentators have sought to portray Thomas as ungallant in some way, someone who wanted all the glory for himself, who was unwilling to acknowledge the enormous contribution Lucy made to the success of the whole venture. Lucy's own book, *Recollections of Tartar Steppes*[1], published in 1863, two years after Thomas died, goes some way to putting the record straight, as she happily recounts her own role in the story and brings in many anecdotes about Alatau, their son born on the Kazakh Steppes.

In truth, this must have been a very difficult burden for Thomas to bear, knowing that he was limited in what he could say and having to write the whole saga in the first person. Ironically, it also meant that his account of the journey is less dramatic

Playing Skakiet by Thomas Atkinson

than it would have been had he included Lucy and Alatau in the narrative. We will return to this subject, but suffice it to say that the rest of this account makes full use of the entries made in Thomas' diaries to help explain the narrative as set out in both *Oriental and Western Siberia and Travels in the Region of the Upper and Lower Amoor*. A close examination of Lucy's book shows that it too is based largely on Thomas' diaries. Time and time again, she follows his account almost to the word, using his phrases, sometimes expanding upon them, but mostly allowing them to carry the narrative. Her book cannot be portrayed as a critique of his, because it is largely based on his diary notes.

Using these materials, it is now possible to put together Thomas' itinerary for his first year of travel. The first half of *Oriental and Western Siberia* does not diverge from the details set out in the diaries. Thus we know that from Yekaterinburg, Thomas first headed north, in the company

of a mining official, towards Bilimbay and the ironworks of Count Stroganov, a member of one of Russia's oldest and most important families, which had been responsible for financing the conquest of Siberia and the establishment of mines and metalworks in the Urals. The next day, after a good sleep and hearty breakfast, Thomas was taken on a brief inspection of the mines and from there to a village on the Chusovaya River, where he embarked in a small boat, hoping to sketch the scenery as he floated gracefully through the countryside. For the next three months he would traverse the Urals before moving on to Barnaul in the Altai and then south for a brief visit to the Kazakh Steppes, beyond the Irtisch River.

Floating down the river, Thomas first visited the mine at Outkinskoi (now Utkinskiy), where around 4,000 men were engaged in making the barges that took munitions from the local factories to Nijni Novgorod, Moscow and St Petersburg.

US Library of Congress

Early photo of Tagilsk with Blagodat Hill in the background

"It was now a scene of great activity," he wrote, *"there being 4,000 men in this small village, brought from various places, all diligently engaged in loading the vessels with guns of large dimensions, made in Kamenskoi Zavod; also with shot, shell and other munitions of war from the different works in the South Oural, destined for Sevastopol and the forts on the Black Sea."*

Thomas notes that on 15 April there was an earthquake *"which caused a great sensation throughout the Ural."* Despite the poor weather, with snowstorms and driving rain, he was struck by the beauty of the river and its setting, noting the curious rock formations. Slowly he made his way down the river, pulling over at night to stay in a village and moving on again the next morning.

The next port of call was Chaitanskoi, where he met friends. But continuing snow storms made progress slow and Thomas

spent a day or two exploring the local area and sketching the river itself. In total, Thomas says he made 28 sketches of the Chusowaya river. In his diary he notes that on 12 July he sent a messenger back to the Foreign Minister, Count Nesselrode, in St Petersburg with a set of 12 paintings of the river, to be presented to the Tsar. In fact, the pictures are still in St Petersburg, in the collection of the Hermitage. And they are a remarkable set, showing Thomas's great skill as a watercolourist. They are, as far as is known, the only set of pictures completed by Thomas.

Thomas arrived at Cynowskoi Zavod, an ironworks belonging to Count Stroganoff, on 29 April. It was from here in 1582 that Yermak the Cossack had set off to conquer Siberia on behalf of the Stroganoffs and to here that he retreated after his initial setbacks. Eventually, on 4th May, Thomas arrived at Serebriansky, an ironworks belonging to the Crown on the small river Serebrianka, where the commander was Leo Nikolayevich

Otrada. The river itself had been dammed to provide a source of power for the ironworks and Thomas mentions that Roderick Murchison had described the same place. Thomas was now, finally, across the Urals and in Siberia. He said he would never forget his journey down the Chusowaya, not least because of a cut on his knee from a fall amongst the rocks on its banks, which "*it seems likely I shall retain through life.*"

From Serebrianka, Thomas made his way towards Kooshwinsk (now Kushva), taking note of the flowers that were beginning to show. Many of them he had not seen before and he added them to his collection. Although none of his flower pictures survive, his descendants say that he completed many such paintings, most of which, sadly, were destroyed in fire in Hawaii in 1922 in the home of his grandson, ALC 'Jack' Atkinson. At the factory here the director noted the state of Thomas' leg and the fact that he appeared to have caught a fever and immediately suggested he should go into what today we would call a sauna. "*After about 40 minutes of drubbing and flogging with a bundle of birch-twigs, leaf and all, till I had attained the true colour of a well-done crawfish, I was taken out and treated to a pail of cold water, dashed over me from head to foot, that fairly electrified me. I found myself quite exhausted and helpless in which condition I was carried back to bed.*" It was eight days before he could get up again.

Once back on his feet he continued his journey, visiting the ironworks at Nijne Toura (Nizhnaya Toura) and then travelling along the Toura valley by carriage to the Katchkanar Mountain. Thomas describes the scene at the ironworks:

> "*All was calm and still in the town, which stands on the south side of the lake; while below and near the rock named 'Shaitan' to the north there were continuous clouds of black smoke, through which tongues of flame and a long line of sparks shot up high into the pure air; these and the heavy rolling of the forge-hammers that now broke on our ears are truly characteristic of this igneous region.*"[2]

Thomas was very struck by the beauty of the area and despite the clouds of mosquitoes, determined to stay for a while and sketch. Reaching the summit of Katchkanar took 11 hours on horseback, where he camped, but slept little due to the humming of the millions of mosquitoes and the smoke from the fire. Thomas found it an inspirational spot: "*Day was rapidly dawning over those boundless forests of Siberia. Long lines of pale yellow clouds extended over the horizon; these became more luminous every few minutes, until at length they were like waves of golden light rolling and breaking on some celestial shore.*"

His ability to describe landscapes, honed by his years as a mason and then architect and refined by his artist's eye, is exceptional. Time and again he brings to life the magnificent vistas that opened up before him. The crags near the summit were thick with magnetic iron ore and in some places cubes or crystals of iron were projecting from the sold rock three or four inches square.

Thomas' next stop was Coushwinsky Zavod, where, together with Austin, he witnessed men wrestling and young girls in local costumes singing and playing games, including a kind of see-saw game called *skakiet* in which two girls at either end of a plank lying across a tree trunk attempted to bounce each other high into the air.

He also decided to climb to the summit of the 1200-foot Blagodat Hill, on top of which is an octagonal chapel dedicated to the memory of a Vogul chieftain called Tchumpin, who according to legend was sacrificed here by fellow tribesmen after he showed the Russians where to obtain magnetic ore. There, on 26th May, Thomas was caught out in a ferocious thunderstorm.

> "*For a few minutes a great dread came over me, knowing that I was standing alone on a huge mass of magnetic iron, far above the surrounding country,*" wrote Thomas, as the storm intensified. "*This was a truly sublime and awful scene – the lightning and thunder were incessant, indeed I saw the rocks struck several times.*"[3]

Further days were spent exploring the valleys and mountains in the district, before on the 3rd June Thomas reached Nijne Tagilsk, a town of around 25,000 people on the banks of the Tagil River and the location of the main metalworks of the Demidoff family. He thought it a well-appointed and prosperous town, with schools, churches, a hospital for the ironworkers and vast warehouses for copper, iron and foodstuffs. "*The smelting furnaces, forges, rolling mills, machine-shops and other works, with their machinery, are on a magnificent scale,*" he commented. Hardly surprising when the extent of metal ore in the region is noted; Thomas says one iron ore seam

Thomas Atkinson's painting of Neviansk, showing the famous leaning tower

was about 80 feet thick and 400 feet in length. Close by were copper mines where huge quantities of green malachite were mined and worked into doors, vases and other grand objects, some of which were exhibited at the Great Exhibition in 1851.

Thomas asked to be shown the malachite mines and was taken down into the galleries, where he saw men at work breaking up a huge deposit of the mineral, estimated at 720,000 pounds in weight. The Demidoff estate here was more than three million acres – larger than Yorkshire – and in addition to the metals already mentioned, there was plenty of gold and platinum (Thomas says he obtained a gold nugget weighing "*more than a quarter of a pound*"). On the 11th June he joined others in a picnic trip to the summit of Biela Gora (White Mountain).

Thomas' next stop was Neviansk, one of the oldest manufactories in the Urals, built by Nikita Demidoff, founder of the dynasty, in the early 1700s. Here he was put up in the Demidoff Castle, which was then a magnificent mansion. "*The rooms have all groined ceilings in brickwork; some of them with ribs and bosses at the intersections, in very good taste, and admirably executed*," he wrote.

Close by was the site for which Neviansk is today most famous – its leaning tower, once used for refining silver, but now a tourist attraction.

Of particular interest to Thomas at Neviansk was the rifle manufactory. "*No rifle made by Purdey (the great London gunsmiths-ed) will carry its ball with more certainty than these*," wrote Thomas and to prove the point he records that two were made for him, by order of the director – one a small bore pea-rifle carrying sixty-four balls to the pound and used for shooting birds; the other a large bore (32 balls to the pound) weapon, used to shoot larger game such as deer, elk, wolves and bears. "*These two rifles cost me – complete with cases and all the necessary apparatus – £4.15s.*"

From Neviansk Thomas travelled southwards via Shaidurikha and Mostovaia and on towards Yekaterinburg, the forest stretching away into the distance, except where it had been cut down to feed the ravenous metal foundries. Beautiful semi-precious stones can be found here: emerald, amethyst, beryl, topaz, tourmaline and garnets. A pair of tourmaline earrings once worn by Lucy and still owned by one of Thomas' descendants probably originated from this region.

Thomas arrived back in Yekaterinburg on 6th July, having completed his tour of the northern Urals. He was struck by the amount of money in the town and the grand mansions, many built with large conservatories where all kinds of tropical plants flourished. The government-owned factories were fitted with machinery made in England, including large steam hammers, lathes, planing machines and drills, all under the control of an English engineer. Nearby was the Granilnoi Fabric (Polishing Factory), where jaspers, porphyry, aventurine and other decorative stones were transformed into columns, pedestals, vases and tables, using water-driven machinery. The pieces made here were of the grandest designs. Thomas says that in 1853 in Yekaterinburg he saw a magnificent jasper table on which four or five men had been employed for six years. Wages were a fraction of those in England:

"*I have seen a man engaged carving foliage on some of the jasper vases, in a style not excelled anywhere in Europe, whose wages were three shillings and eightpence per month, with two poods (or 36lb) of rye-flour per month, to make into bread – meat he is never supposed to eat*[4]."

As a former mason himself, Thomas was undoubtedly speaking straight from his heart. "*There are many men employed in these productions possessing great genius; were they free to use their talents for their own benefit, this country might send into civilised Europe numerous works of vast merit*." He mentions the geological collection he had built up, which by this time already had 72 specimens. He also mentions the many people who helped him – the chief director of mines, the director of the Granilnoi polishing works, the *Nachalnic* (commander), the inspector of hospitals, the mayor and many others. All show that Thomas was given privileged access to those right at the top of society and that, as already mentioned, he was easily able to make friendships. Life here was good, he writes, with the women wearing the latest London and Paris fashions, the best quality food and the finest wines and champagnes on the table – "*the only drawback to comfort being the quantity of champagne the traveller is obliged to drink*". Card playing was very popular, particularly with the women, who usually played for five or six hours a day.

In mid-July 1847 Thomas set off for a tour of the southern Urals, following down the valley of the Issetz River. First he called in on the Syssertskoi Zavod, belonging to the

Salemerskoi family. He describes in detail the layout of the factory and provided details of the proprietor's house, which gives an indication of the style of living that was available to the factory owners:

> *"He is a good musician as well as horticulturist,*
> *and his garden, greenhouses and hot-houses are on*
> *an extensive scale. He has a large orangery, well*
> *stocked with lemon and orange-trees, some in full fruit,*
> *others in blossom giving out a delicious perfume.*
> *There is also a very large house in which cherries,*
> *plums and peaches are grown in great perfection…*
> *His flowers and tropical plants are splendid and well*
> *arranged in several different houses to suit their proper*
> *temperature; in one there was a collection of more*
> *than 200 sorts of calceolaria and almost every plant in*
> *flower. I never saw anything more gorgeous, the*
> *colours were perfectly dazzling and were in all shades*
> *from the deepest purple, crimson, scarlet and orange,*
> *to a pale yellow; these with the beautiful green*
> *of their foliage produced an enchanting effect."[5]*

From here he made his way to Aramil, Lake Silatch, Kasli – famous for its cast iron artistic figures – Lake Irtyash close to Mount Sugomac, and then to Lake Kizil-tash. From here he crossed the hills to Kishtymsky Zavod, with its large Demidoff-Rastorguev Mansion built by the Demidoff family in 1824, but then occupied by the mining director.[6]

Next he visited the Soimannovsky gold mines and Lake Uvaldi before crossing the river Kialim and following its course to Lake Argasi in the Ilman-tou. He then followed the valley of the River Miass, with its luxuriant foliage and birdlife until he reached Zlatoust at the foot of the Urenga, on the banks of the Ay River. Zlatoust, he said, was the 'Birmingham and Sheffield' of the Urals. Ores were smelted in a large blast furnace and then hammered into bars in forging mills before being transformed into steel for weapons manufacture, all under the command of the legendary General Pavel Petrovich Anosov (1799-1851), a scientist and metallurgist, who introduced the production of high-quality Damascened blades and whose flying horse symbol became known throughout the world. The factory is still in existence, producing hand-worked steel.

Thomas met up with Colonel Anosov again the following year in Barnaul, where he accompanied him on visits to some of the

A woodcut of Neviansk based on Thomas Atkinson's' view

zavods in the Altai and again in May 1850.[7] He says that when Anosov died in 1851 in Omsk, the secrets of his metalworking died with him.

From Zlatoust, Thomas made his way to the gold-mining region, where he says many large nuggets had been found, including The Big Triangle, a solid piece of gold found in 1842 at Tsarevo Alexandrovsky that weighs 36kg and is still in existence. He sketched for several days and then travelled to Ah-oosh (Holy Lake of the Bashkirs), at the foot of the Ilman-tou mountain and then on to more goldmines before heading towards Miass across open steppelands. This was Thomas' first experience of open steppe, through which he travelled in a *telega*, a kind of cart. *"The whip was not used once,"* he writes, *"the whole being effected by the driver talking to his horses, they apparently understanding every word. At times he used a shrill call, when the animals would bend to their work like greyhounds; and by speaking to them in another tone, he would bring them up into a canter… From full speed a word brought these fiery steeds into a trot… I have never seen horses in a circus under better control."*

From Miass in the southern Urals, Thomas returned north to Yekaterinburg, where on the advice of local friends, he hired Nikolai, a 24-year-old German servant and failed medical student, whose father was the highest ranked medical officer in the Urals. His friends suggested that the young man would offer some protection against the criminal exiles that roamed the forests in search of plunder. His next objective, Barnaul in the Altai region, was to take him eastwards from Europe and, for the first time, into Siberia proper – a distance of almost 1,900 kilometres.

He left Yekaterinburg at 3pm on the 19th July and passed quickly through Kamensky Zavod and along the Isset River valley. His next significant stop was at the huge Dalmat Assumption Monastery at Dalmatova in Kurgan oblast, close to the junction with the river Techa. It was one of the first Russian settlements in the Trans-Ural region, founded in 1644 by the warrior-monk Dalmat and was, of necessity, built with a large surrounding wall to keep out marauding tribesmen. When Thomas visited, the monk's helmet and hauberk were still held there, but much of the interior was later vandalised during the Soviet era. The monastery impressed Thomas deeply and he praised its architect: "*Most sincerely did I offer up my humble tribute of respect to his genius and memory.*"

Carrying on down the valley of the Isset, the next stop was Shadrinskoi, after which he passed through beautiful country, with fine pastures and woods before crossing the boundary between the regional governments of Perm and Tobolsk. In the Ischim Steppes, for the first time he came across a large party of convicts marching eastwards:

> "*There were 97 in the gang; seventeen men and three women in chains led the van, destined for Nertchinsk, and have yet to march more than four thousand versts. It will take eight months before they reach their place of banishment – they were a most desperate-looking set*".

Every post station on the route to the east included a stockade to hold the prisoners, who left Yekaterinburg every Monday morning.

From Shadrinkskoi the route was via Abatsky, Krutinka, Tyukalinsk and then Beokichevo and into the valley of the great Irtisch river that in turn merges into the Ob. He crossed the river at Serebrenaia and followed the eastern bank of the Irtisch before striking east at Ponstink towards the Altai.

Thomas travelled much of this journey in a *tarantass*, a kind of coach without springs, usually drawn by four horses. The length of the carriage meant that the worst of the impact created by having no springs was mitigated. Passengers usually lay on straw mattresses.

The next stage of the journey, through woods, was known as a spot where robberies were frequent. In preparation Thomas travelled with his pistols drawn from their holsters and caps in place, laid across his lap. He had also bought a double-barrelled pistol for his servant, complete with 11-inch rifle barrels, although he thought it very unlikely that the fellow would have enough nerve to open fire, recording that he would "*gladly surrender the carriage and its contents to secure his own safety*". The *yemtschick* (driver) kept up a full gallop through the woods and before long they were once again in the open steppe. Soon they were in Kiansk, which at that time was mainly inhabited by Polish Jews. He headed south from there in order to visit Lake Sartian and Lake Chany, the latter being the largest in Western Siberia and even though it is shrinking, is still 80 miles by 50 miles in area. The two lakes are the last vestiges of what was once a huge inland sea stretching almost 150 miles to the south.

They were now in the Baraba Steppe, a mostly marshy region that lies between the Irtisch and Ob rivers, where huge numbers of wildfowl congregated and where wild flowers grew in profusion. The going was hard here and three extra horses and three men were needed to get the tarantass along the boggy tracks. Often they had to lay branches along the track to prevent the carriage sinking too far into the mud as they travelled through the night. At last they reached Krutikha on the banks of the Ob, whose source is in the Altai. Now they followed the river valley, which had not long since been under water, reaching Suzun, where there was a copper-smelting works and a mint.

The next stop was at Pavlovsky Zavod, where there was a large silver smelting works, the ore being brought from the Altai. The remains of the works, now overgrown and derelict, can still be found outside the town.

It was now a clear run into Barnaul, which they reached after a journey of 12 days and nights, arriving on the 3rd August. Here

Kazakh horsemen in the Altai in 1880

Thomas, along with Charles Austin, were guests of the director of the mines, Colonel Sokolovsky. "*I slept nearly 12 hours and wishing to take advantage of every day, as the summer was gliding on fast, at 10 o'clock called upon the chief of the mines, who received me with great kindness…he spoke a little English, which was exceedingly agreeable to me; equally so was my introduction to his wife, whom I found a most amiable woman.*" Thomas was to form a close friendship with the Sokolovskys, who were to look after him many times, and came to know Lucy and their son, Alatau, very well. When Thomas decided to head back to Moscow to marry Lucy, it was in a carriage borrowed from the Colonel.

One of the first things Thomas did on arriving in Barnaul was to write a long letter to Lucy. He had written to her from Kammensky *en route* from Yekaterinburg, leaving the letter with the post-house where it would have been picked up by a courier heading in the opposite direction, but he would have been anxious to tell her of his latest adventures. In fact, we can see from his 1847 diary that he wrote to Lucy 66 times during his year away from her. He records in great detail the date of each letter he sent, giving each one a number, recording the place from which he wrote and the day on which he expected her to receive it in St Petersburg.

Seldom did a week go by without a letter being sent – and presumably received, although none of these letters survive. Sadly, we will never know precisely how Thomas courted Lucy via these letters from the vastness of Siberia, but as they were the only form of communication available to the couple, we can be sure that they must have had an strong effect on her, as it was on the strength of what she read that she took the decision to give up her employment as a governess with the Muravyev family and to travel with Thomas in Siberia, despite the fact that she had barely ridden a horse in her life before.

After a few days' rest, on the 8th August Thomas and Charles Austin left Barnaul by tarantass heading south, this time towards the Altai. They were beginning to leave the forests behind and enter into the steppe lands. As Thomas records:

"*These were formerly inhabited by Kazakhs before they were driven back across the river and a line of forts built extending from Omsk along the Irtisch to the River Bouchtarma. These form the frontier to the Kazakh Steppe, which is guarded by Cossacks – the*

whole length of the line, perhaps not less than 2,500 versts, extending far up into the Altai and along the Chinese frontier."[10]

On the 10th August at eight in the evening, after travelling along the valley of the Tchurish (Charysh) River, they arrived at Kolyvan Lake where Thomas, like many visitors before and since, was struck by the curious rock formations, which he sketched. Many of the great explorers, including the Germans Peter Simon Pallas, Alexander von Humboldt and Johann Friedrich Gmelin also passed this way. "*Nowhere else have I ever seen such beauty,*" wrote Pallas. Thomas returned to the lake on several occasions in later years to sketch and admire the views. About 40 miles to the south he could just make out where the foothills of the Altai merged into the Kazakh Steppe.

The following day he arrived in Zmeinogorsk, then the richest silver mine in the Russian empire. As their carriage descended into the valley, they saw dozens of wagons carrying charcoal going down into the valley and dozens more on their way to Barnaul carrying silver ore. A day later on the 12th August he left to visit the Kolyma Polishing factory, but within two days was back in Zmeinogorsk, this time very ill. "*I was carefully nursed,*" he says, "*indeed, treated with the greatest consideration; but what with bleeding, physic and starvation, a great change was soon produced and I was rendered thin enough for any mountain journey. The illness was a great disappointment at the time and worried me much during my eight days' detention.*"[11] In his diary he records "*Still very ill in bed*" for the 16th and 17th, but "*Got up rather better*" for the 18th and 19th. He wrote three letters to Lucy while recovering at the house of the director of the silver mine, who had received instructions from Barnaul to afford him every assistance.

As soon as he was well enough, Thomas left Zmeinogorsk to head into the mountains, along the valley of the river Ouba, then crossing into the Oulba valley before making his way to the silver mines at Riddersk, beneath the Ivanovsky Ridge, which is the source of the Gromotukha (Thunder) River. Here he was able to send two letters to Lucy. From now on Thomas would be on horseback, as carriages were of no use on the rough tracks through the mountains. His party had now swollen to 20 horses and 15 men, five of whom were armed. "*I must own we had rather a bandit-like appearance,*" wrote Thomas. At the first village they stopped, Poperechnaya, the

A group of Mohamed's Kazakhs – see page 67

villagers brought him fresh honey in the comb. These people were probably descendants of escaped Russian serfs who had arrived at the beginning of the eighteenth century. They were extremely hospitable to Thomas and his party.

The route now was via the Koksa Valley, past the lake towards the Karaguy River and then the Arakym River. Thomas stopped regularly to sketch the wild scenes around him and was clearly in his element here, miles from civilisation and surrounded by high snow-clad peaks. He slept outside, wrapped in his cloak and furs and woke one morning to find a hoar frost had whitened the trees. Autumn was on its way. Soon the Kalmucks who lived in this area would be coming down from the high pastures with their flocks, taking up residence for the winter at lower altitude in their *chums*, conical homes made from poles and birch bark. At one point Thomas took his watch out of his waistcoat pocket only to see it drop from its chain due to a loose retaining pin. The watch disappeared over a precipice, but got caught in small bush a couple of yards below the edge. Remarkably, he got his men to tie three reins together and with one end fastened beneath his arms and two men grasping the other, he went in pursuit of his timepiece. "*It was only while riding quietly down the valley seeking our encampment that I thought of the risk I had run,*" wrote Thomas, "*and then it made me shudder. My men seemed powerfully impressed by the incident – it was the subject of conversation during the evening and evidently excited no slight interest.*"

As they ascended the mountain slopes of the Cholsun range the scenery grew more and more spectacular and Thomas was clearly impressed, as von Humboldt had been 18 years before. "*The Urals may be of high importance in respect to mining, but the real pleasure of an Asian journey was only brought about by the Altai*", is what von Humboldt wrote to his sponsor, the Russian finance minister.

Whether Thomas was consciously following in his footsteps is unclear, but he was certainly sticking very close to the routes taken by the great German scientist - who had been the first to suggest that he should travel in Siberia. Every now and then Thomas would peel off from the main group and find a spot from which to sketch. At one point he got his first glimpse of Belukha, the biggest of the Altai peaks, lying towards the south, its double peak surrounded by many other snowy crests. "*Such scenes, and many others through which I have passed, offer most glorious studies to the lover of Nature,*

possessed of sufficient courage to woo her in these sublime regions when bedecked in her wild and gorgeous attire."[13]

It was now the beginning of September and snow had already fallen on some of the peaks. The party was now approaching the Bouchtarma River, which they crossed in a dugout canoe while the horses were swum across. They reached Zyryanovsk, now in northern Kazakhstan, on the 2nd September and rested up the following day, with Thomas and Charles Austin having dinner with the director of mines. This was then the most valuable silver-mining site in the Altai, but today is known mostly for lead and zinc, the silver having been largely worked out. When Thomas visited, more than 2,000 horses were employed in taking the silver ore to the smelting works in Barnaul, almost 1,000 kilometres to the north.

Each day now the weather was deteriorating. It snowed on the 4th and then next day the ground was frozen hard, with a bitter wind. Two days later Thomas rode back to the Bouchtarma to sketch. The following day he was ill and stayed in town, writing a long letter to Lucy. On the 9th he was up at 4.30am to make a journey towards the Chinese border. His intention was to visit the lake of Nor Zaisan, but this was a sensitive area and he needed permission from the Cossack officer in charge of the region. Eventually the colonel commanding the district appeared and agreed that Thomas could pass the frontier and sketch wherever he wished but that the route he proposed to take was now blocked by snow in the mountains. Instead, said the colonel, he should get to Ust-Kamenogorsk and then head south into the steppe, following from one Cossack post to another until he reached the fortress at Kockbouchta.

From Zyryanovsk he reached the fort at Great Narym (Bolshenarymskoye), where all the inhabitants were Cossacks. That evening his party entered the Irtisch valley near where the Narym joins it. "*The river once formed the boundary of the Russian Empire,*" Thomas noted almost wistfully. "*The opposite banks is the Kazakh Steppe, which is gradually being absorbed.*"

At Cheremshanka just before dusk the party got into two canoes, heading downstream to Werchnayan pristan. "*It was a calm and beautiful night without even a breeze to ruffle the water; there was not a sound save the plashing of the oars – all nature seemed asleep.*" They arrived at 2.00 in the morning where the local officer soon had a boiling samovar ready for

Kazakhs with koumis bottle and bowl

them. The next day, Thursday 11th September, Thomas made a sketch of the Irtisch and the mountains through which they had passed during the night. In the distance he could now see the Kourt-Chume Mountains that marked the boundary with China.

This intention was to float down the Irtisch to Ust-Kamenogorsk (now Oskemen), a journey of about 200 kilometres, which usually took 12 hours or so. It was the same route used to take the silver ore from the mines at Zyryanovsk. However, it was not to be so simple. The vessel that had been prepared consisted of two small canoes lashed together five feet apart with a platform about 15 feet by ten built on top. Thomas was very dubious about its seaworthiness and ordered alterations, but having been given assurances, the odd craft was steered out into the middle of the stream, which was more than a thousand yards wide, where it promptly began to sink. Thomas continues:

> "I was watching the changes in the scene, as one mountain peak after another came into view, when suddenly and without any previous intimation, two of the men called out that their canoe was filling fast and that they must make for the shore without a minute's delay. Before we got half way to the bank she was nearly full of water and when within about a hundred yards, the men cried out that she was sinking."

Fortunately, they made it to some reedbeds, where they were able to throw the luggage ashore and then get off the stricken craft.

Back at the *pristan* (wharf), they were able to obtain an ore boat, which was a better prospect. By this time one of the boatmen from the sinking craft had absconded, but not to be outdone, Thomas had one of the locals seized and held on the new vessel. As it pulled away, the deserting boatman mysteriously reappeared and once he had been exchanged for the hostage, they set off downstream. That night was spent in a poor cabin alongside the river crawling with *prussacks* – small cockroaches. The next day they were back on the river, passing the junction with the Bouchtarma River. Possibly for the first time, Thomas saw camels on the Kazakh side of the river. The land here was covered in tumuli (*kurgans*), from which he obtained an ancient copper knife. The next night was spent in yet another cabin, as the rain continued

to fall and the wind rose in intensity. The weather continued to be very bad but by the 13th they had made it to Tulovskoi Simovei, the second winter station on the Irtisch. There were already 15 people in the small room here and Thomas' party added another nine. Unable to fit in to what was a filthy room, Thomas decided to spend the night on the boat. He awoke to a sharp frost, but glad he had not had to spend the night in the squalor of the room on the banks. At 9.30am they set off again, arriving at Oust-Kamenogorsk at 4.30pm, where they were treated very hospitably by the director, who had already received instructions by messenger. That evening he wrote a pair of letters to Lucy.

The following day, Thomas met up again with the Cossack officer he had met at Bouchtarma, who reiterated that he could not travel to Nor Zaisan, but that he could visit a little gold mine almost 100 miles out into the steppe and some ruins in the mountains about 30 miles away. He would have to be accompanied by Cossack guards to keep him safe from marauders. The next day he met up with his escort, consisting of two sturdy-looking Cossacks armed with sabres, muskets, pistols and lances. Another Cossack drove a small telaga. To these were added the Cossack Thomas had brought with him from Barnaul and his and Austin's weapons, which, wrote Thomas, "*were quite sufficient for our defence against ten times the number of Kazakhs, should they venture to attack us to keep up their reputation for plundering.*" On the 16th, for the first time Thomas visited a Kazakh *aoul* (camp) where, he notes in his diary, he found the chief "*a very fine fellow*".

> "He had us put into a yourt, carpets spread and gave us koumis and afterwards tea. He arranged that some of his own horses should take us back and rode a little distance with us. He gave me a whip and I presented him with a knife. His son gave Austin a piece of voilock."[16]

The next day, having finished a long letter to Lucy, Thomas and Austin set off south at 1.00pm into the steppe. To the west about 20 miles away, the Monastir Mountains loomed over the steppes. The distance to the ruins by the river was only about eight miles, where they found several large tombs, consisting of a large basement about 12 feet square and eight feet high. On top there was a small pyramid. Nearby was what Thomas described as a temple – a platform some 17 feet high, oriented north-south with the granite bases of columns still visible. He drew a plan of the place (now lost) and described the broken pottery he found in his diary: "*I found many pieces coloured blue, some red and Austin found one striped red and grey. I also found parts of mouldings and some small ornaments in terracotta. It is somewhat difficult to see if a style of architecture has been employed. All the columns are gone and nothing left on the platform excepting the bases of columns and a few straight slabs of granite that may have been steps; in fact two are in their original position, one at the front entrance and the other I have marked on my plan. On the west side are lying four blocks of granite, one of which has a round hole made into it 15 inches in diameter and 15 inches deep. This may have been the altar on which the victims were immolated. The other three have formed a channel through the wall to carry off the water used in the sacrifice. Altogether this is a most interesting spot and one that affords matter for which speculation as to what people inhabited this place and erected such buildings; in all the valleys there are tombs, square masses of rough stone with a raised part in the centre.*" Speculation about the original builders of these tombs and monuments continues to this day.

On the 19th Thomas caught sight of two wolves. Austin wanted to get a shot at them, but they moved off too quickly. At midday they arrived at a small *priesk* (gold mine) where the Polish director – himself an exile – asked them to stay the night. The director, Baron Mattvei Kovaleski, was living here for the summer with his wife and children and about 80 mineworkers, almost all of whom were Kazakh tribesmen. There was a Cossack picket of eight men a couple of miles away, but this was still dangerous territory with *barantas* (raiding parties) passing by from time to time. The Baron offered to give Thomas horses to visit Nor Zaisan, which was only about 70 kilometres distant. They decided to stay for the night and as he settled in, Thomas began his 50th letter to Lucy. The wind was rising, not made any more comfortable by the gale that was blowing into the room through a broken window. He was up early the next morning to mend his gloves and as he admired the director's three greyhound (*saluki*) pups, the Pole offered him one in exchange for a drawing. He decided on the black one, which he agreed to collect on his return towards Oust-Kamenogorsk.

On Sunday 21st September Thomas was up before the sun. After a quick inspection of the new fort being constructed nearby by the Cossacks, the horses arrived to take them to Nor Zaisan. They left just after midday, their party now consisting of six men with 12 horses. They passed the summit called Kolmack-Tologuy, which looked like a monk's head, with a shaven crown and the rocks lower down bristling out at the sides to form what looked like hoary locks. On the summit were ancient rock paintings of men and animals. From here the full extent of the steppes could be seen at last. In the distance they could see smoke rising which they thought at first was the reedbeds at Nor Zaisan that were on fire. In fact, it was the steppe that was burning, not the reeds. They pulled up at a poor yurt for the night where they found a Kazakh woman with four children, three of whom, wrote Thomas, were very ill. After eating Thomas and Austin took a walk to get a better view of the fire. "*Oh what a picture awaited us. The fire was some 12 or 15 versts distant and extending across the steppe some 20 versts at least, lighting up the country for miles around. After remaining about an hour trying to impress this scene in my memory to sketch it as the earliest opportunity, we walked back to our quarters.*"[18]

The next day again Thomas was up with the sun – "*as usual I had finished my tea ere my companion turned out*", he wrote in his diary, in a jibe clearly aimed at Austin. Once again they set off, finding that the fire had advanced some 15 or 20 versts overnight and was still raging. At midday they arrived at a large aoul. The sheep and goats were arriving to be watered, followed by the horses and then the camels. For the first time Thomas saw a sheep killed, butchered and cooked in the traditional manner in a large iron cauldron, but was not over-impressed: "*The Cossacks dined with the Kazakhs; I did not – having seen the entrails put into the pan after undergoing but a very slight purification.*"

Then it was on again towards the lake. But when he arrived it was a disappointment. So dense were the reeds, which reached well over his head, that Thomas found it hard even to glimpse the water. "*I rode along the shore, through these beds of grass for five or six versts and frequently forced my horse into the water above the saddle flaps, but without being able to get a single peep into the lake.*"[19] He returned to the aoul where they were to stay the night deeply disappointed.

The aoul at Kliee on the shores of Nor Zaisan where Thomas stayed that night was large, with 19 yurts. The local khan had more than 3,000 horses and nearly 300 camels, together with oxen and sheep. "*He was a very gentlemanly little man, dressed in a black velvet kalat, a crimson shawl round his waist, a beautifully embroidered cap on his head and a pair of small high-heeled red leather boots on his feet."* His wife, too, was well turned out, *"dressed in a silk kalat, striped with yellow, red and green, giving her a very gay appearance. She had a cap formed of white calico hanging over her shoulders, a green shawl round her waist and red boots. They had four children and these were running about naked."* [20]

This time Thomas was determined not to miss his supper and when once again a sheep was slaughtered, he made sure that the Cossacks got some of it and boiled it up for him. In his diary Thomas lamented that he could not find his marrow spoon. *"I have carried a marrow spoon all the way from Petersburg and now when I want to shew the use of it I have left it behind. I am greatly disappointed. This really made me laugh as I wanted to display a marrow spoon before people who don't even use a knife and fork, but my vanity is great."* [21]

From this aoul the River Irtisch was only a two-hour ride and the next day, Tuesday the 23rd, the party started immediately after breakfast, riding through the reeds for more than an hour before striking out over the steppe. They got to Kara-tas, a Cossack fishing station on Nor Zaisan close to the Irtisch, but soon returned to their host, who provided them with 11 of his own men as guards for the ride. The party was now 19 men and 27 horses and they left at dusk, aiming to reach Kochbouchta (now Kokpekty). That night they stopped at another aoul, where Thomas made a paper bracelet for a woman in the yurt, *"which pleased her very much"*. They made it to Kochbouchta on the evening of the 24th and were joined by several Cossack officers for the evening. Two days later he arrived back at the goldmine of Baron Kovaleski, where he collected the dog, Jattier ('one who can catch'), that he had been promised.

The following day, Saturday 25th, Thomas witnessed an eclipse of the sun, which lasted for just over four hours. He was introduced to the Baron's doctor, from whom he was able to gather useful information about the country, having been a medical officer at one of the Cossack fortresses amongst the Little Horde of the Kazakhs in the west of the steppes. He was also presented with another dog, this one called Mitaban ('elastic sole'), who was renowned as a hunting dog. The mining season was coming to an end and the many Kazakhs working there – more than 80 – were now packing up their yurts, ready to move on to their winter camps.

"The men had secured their hard-earned money in sashes tied fast round their waists; the keen edges of their battle-axes were examined, the thongs tried to see if they fitted their wrists and then they mounted and rode way." [22]

The Baron too was planning to leave with the season's gold packed into his bags. On an excursion with a lone Kazakh into the nearby Isilksou valley, Thomas realised that they were being watched and tracked by a group of horsemen. As the Baron's party and the gold were due to follow the same route the day after it seemed likely that the horsemen, of whom there were sure to be more, were preparing to lay a trap. That night, back at the mine, the Baron made his preparations, cleaning the guns and loading each rifle with 20 small balls in each barrel. Between them they had 15 barrels, enough to see off a raiding party, they hoped. The arrangements were that the Baron, his wife and daughter, along with the gold should go in one telaga; two other children and two servant-women were in a second and Thomas and the doctor were in the third, each drawn by three horses. In addition there were six horsemen and three drivers. As they approached the valley, everyone was full of trepidation. Fortunately, they made it through with no problem. At one point Thomas and three men made a short excursion to view the nearby Monastir Mountains. Sometime after dark they arrived back in Ust-Kamenogorsk.

After barely a couple of days rest, Thomas was off again, this time with an escort of three Cossacks, heading back across the Irtisch and over the steppes. Late at night they arrived at the aoul of a distinguished old Kazakh, marked with a deep scar on one cheek and wearing a coat of brown horse-skin, with the mane running down the centre of the back. On his head he wore a foxskin cap lined with crimson cloth. His boots were the same colour. Alongside him was his wife, wearing a black velvet kalat and white calico head-dress. They had a large yurt, 25 feet across and ten feet high in the centre. Thomas and two of his Cossacks slept there for the night, wrapped in a fur on the voilocks spread across the ground.

The next day Nikolai, Thomas's German servant, decided he had had enough of the steppe and begged to be allowed to return to Ust-Kamenogorsk to await his master. Then, along with two extra men provided by the old khan, they set off south-west towards the Monastir (Monastery) Mountains.

Thomas Atkinson experiences a baranta – an attack by armed robbers

Having sketched here, the group then set out to find the aoul of Mohamed, a celebrated chief, who was thought to be at the Mantilla rocks, 30 kilometres away to the south. When they arrived there were huge herds of horses and camels nearby, along with sheep and goats. Mohamed himself came out to greet Thomas, taking his bridle and helping him off his horse. Once sat down, the first thing he and his three sons did was ask to examine Thomas' pistols, which he removed from their holsters and stepped outside to give a demonstration on how they were fired. They had not seen firing caps before, having only used muzzle-loading rifles, and were deeply astonished.

Thomas provides a detailed description of Mohamed and his way of life[23], noting his clothing, his hawk chained to a perch, the construction of the yurt, together with its fittings, the method of making koumis and the management of horses. He examined the horse tack in detail, noting the decorated harnesses and saddles, the ropes and thongs, the leather *tchimbar* (trousers) worn by Kazakhs and many other details. This is certainly one of the earliest and most complete descriptions of a typical Kazakh aoul, added to which, Thomas was able to describe the preoccupations of its inhabitants and their way of life. He counted 106 camels, more than 2000 horses, 1000 oxen and cows and 6,000 sheep and goats and remarks that the chief had two further aouls with even more animals.

The following day he set off to sketch at the Monastery Mountains, which he said the local tribes would not stay near overnight. The next few days were spent exploring the area and sketching wherever possible. One night he was awoken at about two in the morning by the sounds of confusion:

> "At first I thought it was the rumbling of an earthquake and instantly sat upright; the sound rolled on, approaching nearer and nearer. Presently it passed and the earth shook – it was the whole herd of horses dashing past at full gallop. Now came shrieks and the shouting of men, from which I at once knew that robbers had invaded the aoul. It was but the work of a moment to seize the rifle standing close to my head and rush out of the yurt, when I beheld the Kazakhs with the battle-axes in their hands, spring upon their horses and dash off towards the place where we heard the shouting."[24]

Thomas had experienced his first *baranta* (raid). He picked up a gun and fired after the robbers as they galloped past and a group of men from the aoul mounted to give chase. But they were quickly back having found that there were three times as many robbers and that they were prepared to defend their ill-gotten gains. "*I deeply regretted it was not daylight,*" wrote Thomas. "*Had it been so, some of these desperate fellows would have bit the dust, as they passed in one thick mass within pistol-shot; and the rifles would have brought them down at a long distance.*" The robbers had got away with about 100 horses. Undeterred, the next day he was off again, in the company of two Cossacks and three Kazakhs. He wore his pistols in his belt rather than in the holsters in case they came across any stragglers from the robbers.

From Mohamed's aoul, Thomas decided to head back towards Oust-Kamenogorsk, stopping at another aoul on the way, avoiding heavy rain and sleet "*so thick that we could not see any object at ten paces off.*" As was the case everywhere he visited on the steppes, Thomas was the object of much attention, with people seldom leaving him alone for long. The next day, with three Kazakhs and five spare horses to enable the riders to change and ride fast, they set off again towards the north-east and the Irtisch, about seven hours away. After enduring several soakings, he felt a fever coming on and by the time the party reached Oust-Kamenogork he could not even get onto his horse without assistance. The Polish baron called a doctor and once again he went through the cycle of sauna baths and bleeding. It was another 11 days before he was strong enough to get up.

Soon after Thomas was invited to a ball at which most of the town's 'society' – about 50 people – gathered to celebrate the birthday of a prominent merchant. He gives a wonderful description of Marie Ivanovna, the wife of the stadt-doctor, whose eccentricities ensured her reputation travelled far:

> "There was one lady sixty years old, who was dressed like a young girl of twenty. Her head was bedecked on one side with white cut-glass beads, on the other with green glass drops, most probably originally intended for chandeliers. On her neck she wore a chain, with a large square brooch suspended from it, also of green glass. She had bracelets on her arms studded with yellow glass; and round her waist a girdle with the same material. With her pink silk dress, grey gloves, yellow shoes and decorations, she was one of the most curiously-costumed ladies I ever met."[25]

Soon after she performed a Cossack dance: "*There are indeed few young girls who could in this accomplishment have excelled this old lady of sixty; I have never seen her equal,*" wrote Thomas.

After a hard journey via Riddersk and Zmeinogorsk, Thomas reached Barnaul on 1st November. The city had been built at the junction of the Barnaulka River with the River Ob, its streets laid out on a grid. Around 9,000 pounds of silver were smelted there annually, as well as almost all the gold mined in Siberia. The latter was cast into bars and every year sent in six caravans to the mint at St Petersburg. It was the administrative centre of the mining industry and the *Natchalnik* – director of mines – lived there, along with the heads of the major departments. According to Thomas the town's leading citizens were not poor:

> "*I must say that the mining population of the Altai are more wealthy, cleanly and surrounded by more comforts than any other people in the Empire.*"

In Barnaul Thomas was to meet a man who became a good friend in the short time they knew each other. Dr Friedrich August von Gebler (1782-1850), a German intellectual and correspondent and collaborator with von Humboldt, was the Inspector of Hospitals for the Altai and was also a distinguished naturalist and collector. He supplied specimens of birds and insects to several museums, including the British Museum in London. He had also travelled extensively through the Altai and had collected a huge herbarium of around 1,200 Altai plants, 15 of them previously unknown. His *Overview of the Katun Mountains, the Highest Peaks of Russian Altai*[26] for the first time described the Mount Belukha glaciers and shows the first map of the region. He located the source of the Katun River and also founded the museum in Barnaul. He was awarded three orders of the Russian Empire for his botanical and entomological discoveries.

Gebler was certainly regarded highly by Thomas, as contained amongst surviving family papers in the Dahlquist Collection is a handwritten 13-page manuscript, probably written by Lucy, entitled "*Survey of the Katun Mountains, the highest peak of the Russian Altai by Dr Frederick Gebler*". This manuscript is a translation of part of Gebler's paper, none of which had ever been translated into English, either before or since. Presumably Lucy was able to make the translation during one of several stays in the city. Speaking of Gebler, Thomas says

he "*spent many happy hours in his company during my first winter in Barnaul. On his journey of inspection to the different mines he had visited many interesting places in the Altai and from him I gathered much information relative to my journey in these regions.*"[27]

Despite its remoteness, Barnaul (population 10,000) seems to have been well provided-for. European wares were easily obtainable, albeit expensive. Thomas found English porter, Scotch ale, French wines, port, sherry and madeira on sale, along with tea, coffee, soap, candles, sardines, cheese, and a large assortment of weaponry. He clearly thought it a delightful place:

> "*Since my first winter in Barnaul, I have visited nearly every town in Siberia; have remained long enough to become acquainted with the inhabitants and have entered into their recreations and pleasures; but in no town have I found the society so agreeable as in Barnaul. They have an excellent band, trained by one of the under-officers, a very good musician and respectable performer on the violin, who received his musical education in St Petersburg; under his direction they executed most of the operas beautifully, and with great effect.*"[28]

By now Thomas had almost completed his first year of travel. Having journeyed east from St Petersburg he had visited the Ural mining districts, the impressive Altai and the north-east of the untracked Central Asian steppes. If anything, at this point, he was an explorer of Central Asia. Once on horseback and out on the steppes he appears to have been in his element, taking whatever chances he could to visit areas never before visited by Europeans and enjoying the company of the nomads he met on the way. He relates to the tribal leaders he meets with humanity, showing none of the arrogance or superiority that marrs other narratives. He also seems to have been very happy with the opportunities he had found for sketching the great vistas and scenes of wild nature that greeted him along his route. Already at the end of this first year he must have had a sketchbook full of ideas that he could bring to fruition over the winter.

Whilst staying in Barnaul Thomas wrote to Lucy at least once a week back in St Petersburg. By the beginning of January 1848 he had written 66 letters to her and, presumably, she had written a similar number back to him. Their romance was flourishing. At some point towards the end of that year – the exact date is not known – Lucy and Thomas decided that they should meet up again. What we know from his diary is that he left Barnaul in a sledge lent to him by Colonel Sokolovsky on 13th January, travelling via Tomsk, Kiansk and Yekaterinburg and arriving in Moscow on the 7th February, after an absence of 11 months. He immediately wrote to Lucy in St Petersburg and she arrived in Moscow at nine in the evening on the 16th February. Two days later, in the chapel of the British consulate, they were married. The entry in the books states:

> " *Thomas Witlam Atkinson, native of Silkstone in the county of York in England, widower, artist by profession, of the English church, and Lucy Sherrard Finley, spinster, late resident in St Petersburg, also of the English church, were married according to the rites and ceremonies of the Church of England this 18th day of February.*"

The entry in the registration book in the Moscow Embassy that records Thomas and Lucy Atkinson's wedding

The witnesses to the wedding were Basil Kapnist, Lisa Kapnist and Euphrasia Morrison. Basil and Lisa were son and daughter of Ivan Vasilievich Kapnist, who was the civilian governor of Moscow and therefore an important public official. The Kapnist family was related to the Muravyevs and it seems likely that Lucy knew them because of her position in the Muravyev-Vilensky household. She refers to them in her own book as "*our friends the Kapnists*". That was the reason they decided to attend the wedding. Lucy says she stayed at their grand mansion on Tverskoye St in Moscow prior to the wedding.

The other witness, Euphrasia Morrison (1811-1902) seems to have lived in St Petersburg with her brother William and his wife, Margaret. William Morrison had married in the same chapel in 1844.

We can only begin to imagine what was passing through the minds of Thomas and Lucy at this point. Lucy had given up a secure position with one of the grandest families in Russia, through whom she had met many of the most prominent figures in the Imperial court. She was now intent on spending the next few years possibly travelling through the wildernesses of Siberia and the Kazakh Steppes. She was not at all used to such a life, having had no experience of horses or living rough. But something about Thomas had undoubtedly caught her imagination and she did not stint in her commitment. We don't know if she had to be persuaded to travel with Thomas, or if she was a willing collaborator in a journey that was to last for the following five years and take them to some of the remotest (and bleakest) places on earth. From everything she wrote in her own book, she seems to have been full of enthusiasm for the journey and seldom departs from a narrative that suggests huge enjoyment and satisfaction with the adventure, although her joy is often tempered with sadness and concern for the plight of the political exiles, whose families she had got to know – including the Muravyevs themselves – during her eight years in Russia.

As for Thomas, for most of his first year he had travelled with fellow Englishman Charles Austin, who knew the ropes and spoke some Russian. But they had gone their separate ways, with Austin heading for Irkutsk, whereas Thomas, after travelling back to Moscow to meet and marry Lucy, wanted to return to the steppes. Was Thomas willing to marry Lucy – albeit bigamously – because she would be able to make his journey much easier? Before seeing Thomas' diaries that seemed likely, and other writers have suggested a utilitarian motive for his decision to marry Lucy. But he is so warm towards her in the diaries that it is difficult to believe that it was not a love match. After all, how did he know she would not be a drag on him, asking to go back at the earliest opportunity and creating all kinds of problems once they got into the remote areas? She had no experience of rough travel, and had barely been out of a city before. Thomas was taking a huge risk and it makes much more sense to

conclude that he was willing to travel with her because he loved her and because she wanted to travel with him, rather than believing he took her along on the grounds that she could be useful to him.   ■

1. *Lucy Atkinson, Recollections of Tartar Steppes*, John Murray, London, 1863.

2. OWS, op cit, p51.

3. Ibid, p69.

4. Ibid, p99

5. Ibid, p111.

6. On 29 September 1957 a major nuclear accident took place at Mayak, a plutonium production site for nuclear weapons and fuel reprocessing, close to Kyshtym. It measured as a Level 6 disaster on the International Nuclear Event Scale, making it the third most serious nuclear accident ever recorded, behind the Fukushima Daiichi nuclear disaster and the Chernobyl disaster. The disaster was covered up, but details eventually began to come out in the 1970s.

7. Thomas notes that the East India Company's Captain James Abbott visited Col. Anosov and paid tribute to him in his book *A Journey from Heraut to Khiva, Moscow and St Petersburg* (W H Allen and Co, London, 1843), in which he noted the quality of his blades, which showed "*a degree of perfection which I have never observed in the workmanship even of the ancients and which certainly cannot be approached by fabrics of any Eastern nation at present existing.*"

8. OWS, op cit, p166. A verst is 1.066 kilometres.

9. Whenever Thomas refers to Kirghiz, he is invariably speaking of the Kazakhs. It was universal in the 19th century to describe all the inhabitants of the steppes as Kirghiz. Only in the twentieth century were Kazakhstan and Kyrgystan created, as part of the Soviet Union. Kyrgyzstan, much smaller than its neighbour, is a mountainous country to the south-east of the great steppe lands and although their language and culture are similar, the Kirghiz and Kazakhs have a different history. Wherever Thomas uses 'Kirghis', I have replaced it with 'Kazakh'.

10. OWS, op. cit. p182.

11. Ibid, p186.

12. Von Humboldt to Kancrin, Omsk 27 August 1829 in A von Humboldt, *Im Ural und Altai, Briefwechsel zwischen Alexander von Humboldt und Graf Georg von Cancrin aus den Jahren 1827-32*, F A Brockhaus, Leipzig, 1869, p88.

13. OWS, op.cit, p210.

14. Ibid, p230.

15. Fermented mare's milk and the preferred beverage for the steppe nomads. Only slightly alcoholic,w it is the staple drink throughout the summer.

16. Felt, used by the Kazakh nomads to make their yurts, as well as boots and cloaks.

17. T W Atkinson, 1847 diary, RGS, SSC/143/1 [1847].

18. Ibid.

19. OWS, op.cit, p258.

20. Ibid, p258.

21. 1847 diary, op.cit.

22. OWS, op.cit, p264

23. Ibid, pp284-289

24. Ibid, p298.

25. Ibid, p315.

26. Published as Vol III of *Memoires des Savans Etrangers*, St Petersburg, 1837.

27. OWS, op.cit, p331.

28. Ibid, p334

Thomas Atkinson's watercolour painting of Neviansk from the lake

Chapter
FIVE

A BAPTISM OF FIRE FOR LUCY

Even before leaving Moscow, Lucy had begun preparing for her journey to the East. Her connections through the Muravyevs, for whom she worked, to the families of other Decembrist exiles led to numerous requests to take things to their relatives. "*During my short stay in Moscow, it became known to the families of many exiles that I was going to visit regions where their husbands, fathers, and brothers had spent more than twenty years of their lives. Each member of these families had something to communicate – a wife, who had stood at the gate of Moscow with an infant in her arms, to take the last look at the husband and the father, as he was driven slowly past; young children who were now men and women, who had been horrified with the clanking of chains when receiving the last embrace; then there were mothers who had gazed with agony on their sons as they passed under the great archway, and were lost to them for ever; sisters who had received the last salute of those so dear, and brothers who had met here and grasped each other's hands, but were destined never to meet again: all these had some message which they wished to be delivered. Nor could I refuse them this pleasure, although it would, I found, entail several deviations from our intended route. Had it been possible to dine a dozen times in the day, I think we should have been compelled to do so, as each family was anxious that we should be their guests.*"[1]

We can scarcely imagine Lucy's state of mind as she contemplated leaving the world she had known for the previous eight years – the grand houses of St Petersburg, the Imperial household, the balls, parties and intrigue – and exchanging it for the wilderness of Siberia. True, there were cultured towns and cities there too, but the isolation created by the huge distances, the overpowering grandeur of nature and strange cultures were all new to her. What had her employer, General Muravyev-Vilensky to say to her when she told him she was planning to marry the strange Englishman who had turned up in St Petersburg the year before? Apparently he gave his

Thomas Atkinson's woodcut of a Kalmuck Shaman

blessing. If so, Lucy must have been a remarkable person. It was not the kind of thing one expected from a governess.

The first stage of Thomas and Lucy's journey, to Yekaterinburg, was scheduled to take them 12 days and nights of near-continuous travel in the sledge borrowed from Colonel Sokolovsky. They left Moscow on the 20th February and travelled east via Petooshka (today Petushki) on the left bank of the Klyazma River, and then on to Nijni Novgorod. Their efforts to get back on the road quickly were thwarted by the town's governor, Prince Ourosoff and his wife, who insisted that Thomas and Lucy stay at least until nightfall when the roads would freeze over again and make it easier for the sledge to move. They eventually got going at 10pm, their sledge running on the ice of the Volga River. A sledge in front of them had gone through the ice, but they were luckier, although Lucy soon found that the bitter wind had begun to cut her face and lips, and took to wearing a muslin cloth over her head in the open sledge.

In Kazan, the next important town, they dined with a Persian professor and his wife and the following day visited Prince Irakly Abramovich Baratinsky, the governor, and later attended a musical concert. At one of the post stations beyond Kazan they met a rather drunken Russian soldier on his way to St Petersburg and Odessa, who told them that he was returning after serving for several years in the Kazakh steppes. He said he had some highly secret maps which he would be happy to show them. Lucy recalled:

> "He placed them on the table with most significant nods and winks, stating they were not permitted to be shown to any foreigner, but out of the deep respect he had suddenly conceived for us, he would allow us to have a peep at them."

He said he would sell them for 40 roubles. On declining the offer, Lucy didn't have the heart to tell the soldier that she had procured exactly the same maps for Thomas a year before in St Petersburg.

On leaving Kazan, they had to travel in the forest to find enough snow for the sledge to move over comfortably. By midnight on 6th March they reached Yekaterinburg where, exhausted, they were put up by an English family, the Tates, whom Thomas had met previously and who owned an extensive iron foundry. They also kept a large yacht on a nearby lake. Fresh linen and a soft bed must have been pure bliss to Lucy, who had little experience of this kind of travel. They were to stay in Yekaterinburg until 21st March, visiting friends and making new acquaintances. Thomas called in again at the Granilnoi Fabric where Lucy also saw the jasper table that was being prepared for the Empress, although she was not entirely impressed: "It was certainly beautiful, but still did not appear worth the time and labour that had been expended upon it." At the Mint she was presented with a newly minted set of coins, set in a small box made especially for them.

They decided to leave their wedding presents with the Tates and spent their last day in the town visiting the governor and director of the Ural factories, General Vladimir Andreyevich Glinka (1837–1856), his wife and their daughters, and taking hot spiced wine with the Tates. General Glinka had also hosted Charles Cottrell during his visit to Yekaterinburg in 1840.[2] Mr Tate presented Lucy with a rifle who recorded the fact:

> "I had already a pair of pistols, which Mr Atkinson bought for me in Moscow, so now we have each evening rifle and pistol practice, as it is advisable for me to be at least able to defend myself in case of an attack being made on our precious persons or effects whilst travelling amongst the wild tribes we shall meet with on our journey. I hope, however, I shall not be called upon to use any of my weapons of defence."[3]

Before leaving they parted company with Nikolai, the servant Thomas had first hired the year before. "The fellow was not to be trusted and Mr Atkinson had always treated him with great leniency", wrote Lucy, who was clearly glad to see the back of him. At 9pm they left for Tomsk, although once again there was little snow on the road and the going was hard. Their next stop was Kaminskoi, where they were welcomed by Madame Gramertchikoff and her son, who they had met in Yekaterinburg. Next, they reached the grand monastery at St Dolomete, also visited by Thomas the previous year.

On 25th March they reached Jaloutroffsky (Jalutorovska) where they went straight to the house of Mattvei Muravyev-Apostol, one of the Decembrist exiles. "I enquired for Muravyev," wrote Lucy. "He said he was the person I required. I told him I had come from Petersburg and gave him my maiden name. I was instantly received with open arms. He then hurried us into his

Mattvei Muravyev-Apostol by N I Utkin

sitting room, giving me scarcely time to introduce my husband. I was divested of all my wrappings, although we stated that our stay would be short. He then seated me on a sofa, ran himself to fetch pillows to prop against my back, placed a stool for my feet – indeed, had I been an invalid and one of the family I could not have been more cared for or the welcome more cordial."[4] It was the first of many similar reactions that Lucy would receive from the Decembrist exiles in Siberia, many of whose relatives she had known back in St Petersburg. As Lucy wrote:

> *" There are several of the political exiles of 1825 living at Jaloutroffsky; they form quite a little colony, dwelling in perfect harmony, the joys and sorrows of one becoming those of the others; indeed, they are like one family."*

Muravyev, whose brother Sergei had been hanged (twice)[5] for his part in the uprising of 1825, was regarded by the authorities as one of the most determined of the conspirators. For the first two years of his exile he was banished alone to the remote forests of Yakutsk in north-eastern Siberia before conditions were relaxed and he was allowed to return to society. *"He is a most perfect gentleman"*, wrote Lucy, *"but there is no doubt that he has great determination of character and I should think, to look at him, years of exile have not changed his indomitable spirit; there was nothing subdued in him"*. Later in life, after he was pardoned in 1856, he became a senior figure in the Russian American Company, which traded between Siberia and the United States.

Before long other exiles had arrived at the Muravyev house. Among those who appeared was "Jakooshkin" and his wife. This was Ivan Yakushkin, another of the most prominent Decembrists. Lucy had messages and gifts for almost everyone who arrived, including a gun for Mattvei. Another woman, widow of a Decembrist, was asked by Lucy on behalf of relatives if she would agree to send her two children back to St Petersburg to be educated. The assembled party then settled down to exchange information. Thomas and Lucy brought news of the February Revolution in France, details of which had just reached Moscow as they were leaving and which must have cheered up the exiles. *"They were greatly excited and many were the speculations as to how it might end. It probably brought to their minds scenes and events in which they had acted a part years ago,"* Lucy wrote. As democrats, the Decembrists identified with the aims of the French revolutionaries, who ushered in the Second Republic. Another

of those who turned up was 'young Bibikoff', possibly the son of Mattvei's sister, who was on his way to St Petersburg. On leaving, the Atkinsons were given several English books to read on their journey and made to promise to return on their way back to St Petersburg.

This was Thomas' first meeting with any of the Decembrists. It must have been a slightly odd situation for him. He was, after all, travelling on a personal passport signed by the Tsar. Nicholas I was a deep reactionary who pulled back from many of the reforms that had been considered by his elder brother Tsar Alexander I, and who consciously decided not to allow the emancipation of Russia's serfs – slaves in all but name. And yet under Lucy's influence here was Thomas meeting and socialising with the very men – now in exile – who had been responsible for attempting to overthrow Nicholas and bring about a constitutional democracy. Thomas was to be deeply affected by his meetings with the Decembrists – and their wives who had heroically followed them into exile, giving up their lives of luxury in St Petersburg to live in the wastes of Siberia. One of the last things he ever wrote, in 1861, and now preserved in the Dahlquist Collection, is a draft contract for a final book, to be called *The Exiles of Siberia*. By the time they returned to St Petersburg in December 1853, the Atkinsons had probably met more of the exiled Decembrists than anyone else alive at that time.

After more adventures on the road, including becoming stuck fast in the snow, they arrived in Omsk at 4pm on 27th March where the local police master treated them very badly and directed them to a common lodging house on the outskirts of the town. They survived the night, and the following day Thomas went to see Prince Peter Dmitrievich Gorchakov (1790-1868), the governor of Western Siberia, to present his papers. Gorchakov asked to see Thomas' paintings which were shown later in the evening to a large gathering. Thomas presented one of his pictures to the Prince and promised to send him another large painting showing a view of the River Irtisch. The Prince asked to be forgiven for not inviting Lucy, explaining that it was because he had no other women available to join the party. The next day the Prince ensured that Lucy was invited to dinner, even though he only had his staff in attendance. He also agreed to allow the couple to travel south through the steppes to the newly-founded town of Kapal in the shadow of the Alatau Mountains and also handed Thomas a map of the steppes and a letter of introduction to the governor of Tomsk.

Among those they met in Omsk was Baron Silverhelm[6], the head of the topographical department, and his wife, who urged the couple to come back and stay with them for a few weeks. Soon they were off again, heading towards Tomsk, which Thomas wanted to reach before the river ice began to break. At the village of Kaiansk he found his dog Jattier, who had been lost on the journey to Moscow.

Soon after this they were in for an unpleasant surprise. Pushing on through the night, they were on a long haul of more than 30 kilometres and both Thomas and Lucy fell asleep, only to be awoken at one in the morning by the sound of the dog growling and the realisation that they were not moving. As Thomas awoke, the first thing he noticed was that the horses were nowhere in sight.

" *On looking out I saw two of the horses were taken off. Instantly I jumped out and found four men standing by the sledge, but no driver. Nor could I see the horses anywhere. There were three or four small cottages, but no station. Lucy asked for the man. They knew nothing about him. Nor would they lend us any aid. They began to be very impertinent. I walked round the sledge and got out my pistols as I disliked their proceedings. I now walked up to them feeling secure and demanded horses. This they treated with contempt. I then desired Lucy tell them I must have horses instantly, but this had no effect. I cocked the locks of my pistols and Lucy told them I would shoot the first man that attempted to run off or do anything excepting getting horses ready. The click of my pistols had a magical effect instantly. Horses were found and a man on the sledge to drive. I then jumped in and away we went glad to get out of such despicable company. No doubt my pistols saved me.*"[7]

Lucy adds: "*There is no doubt our yemtschick had perceived we were asleep, as the sledge was not closed on account of a feeling of suffocation, which always came across me when it was, and that he took the opportunity of driving us into the forest, intending at the least to rob, if not murder us. As we drove away from this horrid place, we observed him peeping out from behind the trees*"[8]. It was not to be the last time the Atkinsons would have to draw their weapons.

As they approached Tomsk, the snow was becoming thinner and thinner. They finally arrived on 4th April, glad not to have

to travel any further with a broken runner, which Lucy said reminded her of sailing over a rough sea. They were put up in the governor's residence even though he and his family were in Barnaul. With the roads now in very poor condition, they were to be stuck in Tomsk for more than a month, until the roads had dried out sufficiently to pass on to Barnaul. The only public dining room in the town was run by a German giantess and a dwarf albino who had once been part of a travelling circus: "*These two, weary of the life they were leading, agreed to marry and settle down, she being an excellent cook, and he a good hand at making port wine*", wrote Lucy.

Having arrived just before Easter, there were plenty of balls and parties taking place in the town and Thomas and Lucy set about meeting as many people as they could. They befriended the Asterhoffs, who owned gold mines along the Yenesei River and who showed them two enormous nuggets weighing 25lb and 30lb. They also met Dr King, who practised medicine in the town, and another Englishman who had been sent into exile for forgery – a charge which he said had been fabricated. The parties seem to have been grand affairs according to Lucy:

" *Amongst the guests there was no mistaking the wives of the wealthy miners. They were dressed with good taste – you will say, where is the Russian who does not dress well? – and wore a perfect blaze of diamonds.*"

Lucy describes one dinner party for 40 guests which consisted of 14 courses. When the guest of honour, the local archbishop, tried to leave after the sixth course, the hostess, worried that everyone else would leave the table which had been eight days in preparation, was able to persuade him not to, mainly by encouraging him to drink more. Eventually the drunken prelate fell asleep.

They eventually left Tomsk on 3rd June at 8.00am. Before leaving the Asterhoffs presented Lucy with a beautiful rifle made by Orloff in St Petersburg. By this time most of the snow had gone and the countryside was covered in the most beautiful wild flowers – globe anemone, forget-me-nots, deep blue iris and many others. When Thomas had passed this way in January there had been 43 degrees of frost. Now the main problem was flooding. Often they were moving along through water that reached up to the axles of their carriage. When they eventually reached the valley of the Ob on the 6th June, they could see it had overflowed the banks and in places was more than 20 kilometres wide. Lucy says that they had been plagued by mosquitoes as they approached the Ob, made much worse for them by the lack of a breeze and their slow progress due to the flooding. In desperation for some wind, Lucy suggested that Thomas should try the "sailor's remedy" (urinating) when overtaken by a calm. This he did and in no time a strong wind had sprung up, which turned into a fierce storm that prevented them crossing until the following day – and even then it took three hours. The spent the night huddled in their carriage. "*It gave us something to laugh at, and I made a promise never to be caught meddling with the wind again,*" wrote Lucy.

On the 7th June, once they had crossed the Ob, it was a comparatively short ride to Barnaul, where they made for the house of Thomas' friends, the Strolemans, who were delighted to put them up for as long as they wanted. The next day began a series of introductions, where Thomas showed off his new wife to the friends he had left almost six months before. There was Madame Anosov, the wife of Major-General Pavel Petrovich Anosov[9], the governor of Tomsk, and Madame Sokolovsky, wife of the director of mines for the Altai, along with Madame Kavanko. That evening General Anosov and Col. Sokolovsky returned from their trip. Lucy presented the colonel with one of Thomas' pictures of Kolyvan Lake in the Altai as a thank-you gift for the loan of the sledge which Thomas had used to travel to Moscow and back. The next day General Anosov was presented with a watercolour of the Ouba River. "*The General said I had painted Siberia as it is, that there was nature in all my works and not fancy,*" Thomas recorded in his diary.

Lucy was forced to take to her bed soon after this, suffering from the effects of the hard journey they had just made. A Tartar woman was brought in to bleed her but it was not until a week later that she was up on her feet, ready to take part in the social life of this busy little town of 10,000. On Sundays everyone gathered for lunch at the Sokolovskys, returning again for supper in the evening, when there would be dancing and cards. On Wednesday nights one of the officers would organise a soirée. They would gather around Thomas, who would regale them with tales of his travels. There were picnics and mushroom-gathering expeditions and shooting parties for the men, who were always copiously supplied with champagne and wines. Thomas says there was an excellent

band in the town and three ladies who played pianoforte. In the winter, when many officers returned from distant outposts in the mountains, there were balls and concerts.

Thomas left Lucy in Barnaul for several weeks while he and Colonel Sokolovsky went on a snipe shooting expedition along the Mrassa River and then on to the upper part of the Tom where the Colonel was due to inspect the gold mines. She knew that Thomas was due at some point to make a trip to Lake Altin Kool (now known as Lake Teletskoye) and the other women of Barnaul tried very hard to discourage her from making the trip. "*They say it is ridiculous,*" she wrote, "*the idea of my going, as the gentlemen get thoroughly knocked up who have ventured so far; however, I have a little wilfulness in my disposition, and am determined to try, and it will be rather odd if I do not succeed. One lady says I may be able to ride one or two days, and she will even give me three, but more it is impossible to do; so they expect me to return alone.*"[10] How wrong they were!

On 9th July, two days after Thomas returned from the Mrassa River, they set off from Barnaul for Bisk and then on to Lake Altin Kool. Before leaving Thomas arranged to meet Colonel Sokolovsky in Zmeinogorsk and to leave their spare baggage with him, carefully listed in his diary. Thomas lost his *tchube* (fur cloak) on the way, but a Cossack sent back to search for it, found it lying by the road. In Bisk they were met by Colonel Keil, commander of the Cossack detachment, who was very helpful and provided useful information on the steppes. His wife, deputed to look after Lucy, was less endearing: "*From her I would defy anyone to gain information upon any subject, excepting it might be dirt! And on this point I fancy her information would be original.*"

On leaving Bisk they were travelling along hills that overlooked the valley of the River Bïa, which flowed out of Lake Altin Kool. It was a hard journey. Their next stop was Sandyp on the 12th July, which was occupied by Cossacks and their families only. From now on they would have to travel on horseback as the track was too difficult for carriages. This meant jettisoning yet more of their clothing and equipment, to be picked up on their return. The following day as they left the village they were followed by the Cossack women. Lucy recalled: "*One old woman with tears had entreated me not to go, no lady had ever attempted the journey before. There were Kalmuck women living beyond, but they had never seen them. In the early part*

Thomas Atkinson's watercolour of Lucy and her guides on lake Altin Kool

Lake Altin Kool by Thomas Atkinson

of the day she had offered to let her daughter go to take care of me; however, when the daughter came in, a healthy, strong girl, some thirty-five summers old, she stoutly refused (to my delight) to move; the mother tried to persuade, and did all she could, it was of no use; and I was left in peace."[11]

Lucy says that she brought a beautiful side saddle with her from Moscow but when Colonel Sokolovsky had seen it, he had warned her against its use, saying it would be no good in the mountains. Instead, he lent her one of his own, about which she had no regrets:

> "*At times, we have had ledges of rock to ride round, where, had I had a side-saddle, my legs would have been crushed to pieces or torn off. At times, I have had to lift my feet on to the saddle, there being barely room for the horse to pass between high masses of rock. Then there were passes to ride over, formed by the granite mountains, in places quite perpendicular down to the Bïa. Our horses have stood on many points, where we could see the water boiling and foaming probably 1,000 feet below us; just imagine me on one of these places with a side-saddle!*" [12]

So, unusually for the time, she rode *en cavalier*, wearing trousers rather than a skirt.

The next day, they rode all day until eight in the evening, at which point their Cossacks built them a *balagan* – a kind of shelter. Lucy says that by hanging a sheet up at the open side, she was able to undress. She was less impressed by Thomas' habits and soon told him so:

> "*I now found that Mr Atkinson had been in the habit of sleeping amongst these wandering tribes without doing so. I told him, without undressing I should soon be knocked up, and advised his following my example, which he did, and continued doing so with benefit to himself.*"

By this time, in early July, Lucy must have known that she was pregnant. And yet she never mentions the fact in *Recollections* until the birth has actually occurred. Did she keep it secret from Thomas, anxious in case he sent her back to Barnaul? That seems likely, as his diary too mentions nothing about her pregnancy. For the first few days on horseback she found

the going hard, but, as she says, "*I determined to conquer this weakness*". Soon she was riding like a veteran.

Their party now consisted of a *talmash* (translator), a Cossack and five Kalmucks, plus eleven horses. By Wednesday the 14th they had reached a Kalmuck village beyond the River Lebed, having travelled 65 versts that day. The next day, as they neared the summit of some high granite rocks, Lucy's horse stumbled and she almost fell, but managed to keep her seat, much to the admiration of the Kalmucks. In another 50 versts they reached another Kalmuck village where they witnessed a remarkable scene. As they sat eating dinner, they saw a young girl running towards the River Bïa, pursued by a man on a horse, with others following on foot. As soon as she reached the river bank, the young girl threw off her headdress and leaped into the water, where she was swept downstream. Two men following along the bank jumped in and one of them pulled her out, still alive. It transpired that the man on horseback was her brother and that she had jumped into the river to avoid being married off to an old man she did not love. The young girl survived, but the Atkinsons never found out who she married.

A similar event occurred the following day, but this time Thomas was asked to exercise the judgement of Solomon. In a Kalmuck village they found a group of men surrounding an old woman, and, a short distance from them, a group of girls assembled around a very pretty young girl of about 16, who appeared quite unconcerned, and was busy cracking nuts. She was the woman's daughter and the six men were all suitors, one of whom the mother thought a good match.

Thomas was asked to decide the case, with each man pleading his cause. Lucy says that the most eloquent of all was an old man, who spoke of his possessions, his lands, his herds of cattle, his position as the chief of the village, and finally of the great love he had for the young girl. Thomas listened as all the speeches were translated and then asked the young girl to step forward. He asked her, through the interpreter, which of the suitors she preferred. She resolutely rejected all of them, as a result of which Thomas suggested that it would be better for her to remain with her mother until she found the man she wanted to marry. "*The lovers retired satisfied, since no one had obtained more favour than the other,*" wrote Lucy. "*The young girl thanked Mr Atkinson*

Thomas and Lucy Atkinson's camp on Lake Altin Kool. They can be seen on the right of the painting

by a smile, but the mother looked disappointed, as she had pleaded for the old man, whose age appeared more suited to the mother than to the daughter, he being the old woman's senior by many years."

A day later, on Saturday the 17th July, an incident occurred that was undoubtedly a great test for Lucy. Faced with very steep cliffs, they decided to take the horses around a point that jutted out into the river, which here was a torrent. There was a narrow ledge, but even so, the water was up to the horses' saddleflaps. One step away from the rock was deep, fast water. As Thomas records in his diary:

> *"All passed well except Lucy. The Cossack who led her horse did not keep him close to the rock. In two or three steps he was in deep water and swimming. Our guide saw this and called to the Cossack to hold the horse just by the bridle or they would both be lost. Lucy sat quite still (tho' the water filled her boots) and was drawn round the point and landed in safety. This was truly a most dangerous place."*

Lucy recalled that an old Kalmuck woman who had joined the party screamed out as she languished in the deep water. But her calmness and decision to sit still as the Cossack grabbed hold of the bridle saved her. Thomas makes no mention of this event in his book, merely stating that *"after a difficult and sometimes dangerous ride on horseback over a wild mountain region, we made our first night's lodging in a balagan on the Altin Kool or Golden Lake"*[13], but his diary notes make clear his admiration for Lucy. Not for the last time did his narrative lose something through his decision not to tell anyone about Lucy.

A close-up showing Thomas and Lucy in their rough shelter

They reached the Lake that evening, just as the sun was setting and camped close to where the River Bïa debouches from the Lake and near the present-day village of Artybash. It was a magical moment for Lucy: *"It was one of the most lovely scenes that could well be imagined; a bright sun shed its light over lake and mountain; the water was calm and shining like molten gold, in which* the rocks, trees, and mountains were reflected as in a mirror, redoubling the beauty of the scene. We sat on our horses looking at this picture for a long time, enraptured by its beauty. It repaid us well for all our toils, and, when contrasted with the rugged scenes we had passed over, this was like enchantment; and still more so as I looked around, for mountains rose up on every side, with apparently no outlet: it was as if we had been dropped down from the clouds into fairy land."*[14] This scene also complements the sepia-tinted lithograph entitled *'Altin Kool, Altai Mountains,'* that appears in *Oriental and Western Siberia*.[15]

To this day, Lake Teletskoye, as it is now called, is regarded as one of the great natural beauties of the Altai region and is part of a World Heritage site. Almost 80 kilometres long, 5 kilometres wide and surrounded by high mountains, it is over 365 metres deep in parts. Lucy was almost certainly the first European woman ever to visit the lake.

That evening Thomas and Lucy took a boat to the other side of the lake to a headland from where he could sketch. On their way back Thomas decided to start playing his flute, which he carried with him throughout his travels. The sound of the flute had an almost magical effect on the local Kalmucks, many of whom had arrived to look at the strangers. As soon as he got out of the boat, Thomas was surrounded by them, begging that he should continue to play. *"The power he gained over these simple-hearted people by his music was extraordinary,"* wrote Lucy.

> *"We travelled round the lake in small boats, it was a tour of eleven days, and in all that time he never once lost his influence; like Orpheus, he enchanted all who heard him; without a murmur they obeyed him in everything; indeed, there was often a dispute to ascertain which might do his bidding; and there was no lack of hands to spin the line which was required to sound the lake."*

By now their party consisted of two Cossacks, the talmash (translator) and 11 Kalmuck boatmen and the next day they set out to explore the lake in five canoes, some of them fastened together. They were caught in one of the many storms that sweep across the lake and had to put in for safety. It was an unpleasant surprise for Lucy, who said she had never experienced anything like it before. Their campsite was recorded by Thomas in a remarkable painting that is now at the Royal Geographical Society. *A night scene at our encampment on the Altin Kool, Altai Mountains*[16], shows Thomas and Lucy resting under an open-sided shelter, while their Kalmucks are gathered round a raging fire. Lucy described it thus:

> "*We went for a short walk along the shore; on returning, and as we drew near our bivouac, one of the wildest scenes I had ever witnessed came into view. Three enormous fires piled high were blazing brightly. Our Kalmuck boatmen and Cossacks were seated around them, the lurid light shone upon their faces and upon the trees above, giving the men the appearance of ferocious savages; in the foreground was our little leafy dwelling, with its fire burning calmly but cheerfully in front of it.*"

Lucy took the opportunity to improve her marksmanship in the forests surrounding the lake. She now had four weapons: a small rifle given to her by Mr Tate, the Orloff shotgun presented to her by Mr Asterhoff and a pair of pistols she kept in her saddlebags. When she shot a squirrel, a Kalmuck begged her to allow him to have it for his supper, which she agreed to as long as she could have the skin. She says that the Kalmucks were not too fussy about what they ate, even eating the odd lynx that Thomas shot.

One night around 20 Kalmucks came into their camp and sat around the blazing fire. Soon their arms were slipped out of their fur coats and they sat with their entire upper body exposed, their ponytails hanging down from the back of their heads. At one point a brawl almost broke out over some small pieces of coloured silk Lucy had given to some of the men, not helped by the fact that many of them were drunk. The couple were relieved when, shortly before midnight, the group upped and left.

Lucy was clearly enchanted by the lake and remarks that in years to come they would recall the happy times they had experienced there. This was her first real experience of outdoor adventure – riding horseback, camping in the wild, relying on the countryside for food – and she relished it. She would never lose her enthusiasm for rough travelling, even under the most difficult circumstances. After 11 days, having thoroughly explored the lake and having completed a circumnavigation, they set off back along the Bïa River, making a raft at one point and then gliding gracefully back to Sandyp.

Their next objective was to be the Kazakh steppes, where they hoped to reach the distant settlement of Kapal. First, they travelled via the Katun River valley through the mountains on a journey that took almost three weeks, often riding well above the snowline. At one point they got their first views of Mount Belukha, the grandest of the Altai Mountains, "*looking like a ruby encircled by diamonds*", as Lucy described the peak. This was very difficult and dangerous terrain, but the horses were magnificent, despite the fact they were unshod. Having reached the village of Kokshinska late at night, Lucy was exhausted:

> "*I had been so many hours on my horse, and had passed over such frightfully difficult roads, that when we stopped, I was actually obliged to be led, for I could not stand, my limbs were so benumbed. After lying on the bench in the cottage for a few seconds, I recovered. There was no possibility of giving way to fatigue on this journey; I had all kinds of duties to perform. The next day, after bathing, I was all right again. I have generally been able to bathe every morning and evening this summer, and sometimes in the middle of the day; without doing so, I do not believe I should have accomplished the journey half as well.*"[17]

A young girl in the village refused to believe that they had come down the mountainside at night, saying it was near impossible, even during the day.

Their intention was to travel on to Belukha and get as close as possible to the summit. But on the 3rd August they reluctantly decided to turn away, hoping to return another day. By now snow was starting to fall and they would certainly have perished if they had pushed on. Instead they continued to descend the Katun River and then across the Yabagan steppe, where they found a Kalmuck aoul and a shaman, who beat his drum for them. Thomas sketched him, although the old man thought that his spirit was in danger of being captured.

After many days riding through the mountains, finally, on 26 August, they made it to Zmeinogorsk, where they stayed at the house of Colonel Gerngrose, who was known to Thomas and who was director of the silver smelting works. For the first time since Barnaul Thomas and Lucy slept in a bed: "*Oh what a luxury it seemed to be, and how I enjoyed it*", Lucy wrote.

A week later, at 7pm on 2nd September, they set off once again, this time heading for Semipalatinsk (now Semey in Kazakhstan). By midday the next day they were on the banks of the Irtish River, crossing it by moonlight that night. It was 6am on Saturday the 4th September when they reached Semipalatinsk, where Thomas showed his letter from Prince Gorchakov to the police master, who said he had already received orders from the Prince. The following day they began what was to become an epic journey, heading for the distant Cossack outpost of Kapal, 1,000 kilometres away to the south.

Why Thomas had chosen Kapal as his destination is not clear. He may have heard about it from some of the military officers they met on the way. Or it may have been suggested by Colonel Sokolovsky or General Anosov, who would have known about the Cossack expedition the previous year that first reached the small encampment lying on the plain beneath the Alatau Mountains. They had sent a battery of mountains guns to protect the encampment and only weeks before a larger expeditionary force of Cossacks, together with their wives and families, had set off on the long march southwards. It was not an easy journey and several of the Cossacks had died on the way, as Thomas and Lucy were to see for themselves, when they came upon their graves in the steppes. Whatever the reason, they were now well on their way. Thomas was, by this time, already a seasoned traveller and had already the year before followed much of this route down to the Kazakh steppes. He was confident and experienced.

For Lucy it was a completely different experience. Although she had now been in the saddle for two months, travelling hundreds of kilometres across very rough terrain, this was still new to her and her pregnancy must have made this a particularly hard journey. And yet she showed no signs at all of backing out. In fact, very much the opposite. She appears to have relished the journey and only seldom loses her sense of fun and adventure on what was to become the toughest journey of her life.   ■

1. *Lucy Atkinson, Recollections of Tartar Steppes*, John Murray, London 1863, p1
2. Charles Herbert Cottrell, *Recollections of Siberia in the Years 1840 and 1841*, John W Parker, London, 1852, p340.
3. *Recollections*, op cit, p21
4. Ibid, p23
5. The first time the rope broke and when he came round, Sergei was told that another rope had been sent for. At which point he said *"it was very hard for a man to have to die twice"*. Soon after he was duly despatched. Another brother, Hypolyte, had killed himself after being arrested.
6. According to Petr Petrovich Semenov, in 1856 Silverhelm, along with Col. Khomentofski, were the first outsiders to set eyes on Lake Issyk Kul and the snowy peaks of the Tien Shan in modern-day Kyrgyzstan.
7. RGS, Thomas Atkinson Collection, 1848 diary.
8. *Recollections*, op.cit, p33
9. Thomas had met him in the Urals the previous year.
10. *Recollections*, op.cit, p47
11. Ibid. p53
12. Ibid. p54
13. OWS, op. cit, p363
14. *Recollections*, op.cit, p62]
15. OWS, op. cit. opposite p363.
16. RGS, 700114. The painting, along with three others held by the RGS, once belonged to Sir Roderick Murchison.
17. *Recollections*, op.cit, p76

Chapter
SIX

DESERTS AND SNOWSTORMS

Thomas and Lucy set off south from Semipalatinsk in what is now northern Kazakhstan, across the vast steppe towards the Alatau Mountains on 6th September 1848. The road then, as today, runs almost due south through a desolate landscape of scrubby grass, rocks and salt lakes.

The travelling was hard and they managed only five versts an hour and had to stop frequently to rest the horses. Lucy says that at times it required eight horses to drag the carriage out of the bogs, which had been made worse by overnight rain. On the 7th they saw the Arkat Mountains in the distance and by midday had made it to the Cossack picket, where Thomas sat down to sketch. A lithograph of his drawing can be seen in *Travels in the Region of the Upper and Lower Amoor*. Little has changed in this area in more than 160 years. There are few habitations, the road is poor and there are few, if any, signs of cultivation. The nomad yurts, visible in Thomas' watercolour,

are long gone, although the return to Kazakhstan in recent years of Kazakhs who had fled across the Tien Shan to China, has seen a small influx of people who still lead a semi-traditional lifestyle.

On 9th September Thomas and Lucy arrived in Ayaguz, a fortress and home to 800 Cossacks, but now without artillery, which had been sent further to the south. The commander was away, but once again the officer in charge had already been informed of their impending arrival. In the morning they got ready to move out, this time on horseback, leaving their carriage in the care of a Cossack officer. Now, in addition to Cossacks, they were accompanied by a group of Kazakhs, who Thomas said had a "strong and wild appearance". The terrain was now sand and low hills, with little vegetation. That night they slept in a Kazakh aoul on the bank of a small stream in a yurt erected for them under the direction of their Cossack

Thomas Atkinson's lithograph of the Arkat Mountains, surrounded by salt lakes

Peter. Their host was a wealthy Kazakh who decorated the yurt with voilock and beautiful carpets. A sheep was killed and cooked in a large cauldron. Thomas says this was the first place they saw sheep being milked.

On Friday 10th September camels were added to the Atkinsons' baggage train for the first time, which now consisted of three Cossacks, five Kazakhs, plus the Kazakh host and his attendants. From here the land took on an even more desolate character, with no trees or bushes or any sign of vegetation. West of them lay a large saline lake, which Thomas names as Yakshe Kessile-Tuz, surrounded by red vegetation, indicating its salinity. This lake, which now exists largely as a saltpan, is one of many vestigial lakes that are the remains of a watercourse that once linked the giant Lake Balkhash further westwards, to Lake Sassykol ('Smelly' lake), Lake Alakool and Lake Ebinur in Western China.

At this point, Thomas' host appears to have got lost. "*Our host was now at a loss which way to proceed to find an aoul,*" he says in his diary. They rode on, coming across many tombs, some of considerable size, built in stone in a conical form. Some of these tombs can still be seen in the same region. Travelling this road in the summer of 2015, I was surprised at the shapes and sizes of these tombs. They were, not built by the Kazakhs, said Thomas, but by a people "*swept away ages ago.*"

In some places, efforts have been made in recent years to repair and replace the ancient tombs that can be found along some of the old trade routes. Just outside Kapanbulak, for example, can be found the Mausoleum of Kengirbay Zhandosuly, also known as Bi Ata. Born in 1735 and a member of the Argun tribe of the Tobykty clan of the Middle Horde, his life is celebrated in many local poems and songs. The first mausoleum was built in 1825. This was replaced by a newer edifice in 1996 and a magnificent new limestone building was under construction in September 2015.

In *Travels…* Thomas says that the journey from Ayaguz south to the River Bean and the Kara Tau mountains that marked the southern boundary of the Kazakh Steppes took him about 10 days. It was, he says, the boundary between the pastures of the Great and Middle Hordes – two of the three hordes (*jus* in Kazakh) that make up the population, even today. He passes over these ten days briefly, noting only that the country "*varied greatly in its aspects. Arid steppes were frequently crossed, on*

which the grass was withered by the sun and the only patches of green were the salsola bordering the numerous salt lakes." In fact, this journey was almost a complete disaster and it is only by the slimmest of chances that Lucy, now more than six months pregnant, made it at all. To find the full story, we have to rely on Thomas's diaries and a few references in Lucy's book.

Lucy writes that the Cossack women she met in Ayaguz advised her strongly against attempting the journey south to Kapal. Her response was remarkable:

> "*They had heard of the great horrors and miseries endured by some of the wives of the Cossacks who had but lately crossed the steppe with their families on their way to the new fortress. They were convinced I should die ere I reached the place. I laughed at their fears, and assured them that it would cause me much anxiety to be left behind, and, even though they told me that death would be my lot if I went, still I was firm to my purpose. You know I am not easily intimidated when once I have made up my mind. I started on this journey, with the intention of accompanying my husband wherever he went, and no idle fears shall turn me; if he is able to accomplish it, so shall I be. I give in to no one for endurance*".[1]

The ladies of Ayaguz prepared bread and salt for Lucy, little meat pies and an enormous water melon. She set off with "*a great waving of caps and handkerchiefs*". At their first stop Lucy was to have her first experience of the real steppe life. She describes "*Herds of cattle were seen in every direction, men and boys on horseback engaged driving them towards the aoul, and a still stranger sight, women busy milking the sheep.*" It must have been an overwhelming sight, later sketched by Thomas.

Having described the hospitality of the Kazakh chieftain already mentioned by Thomas, she describes the difficulty of the journey. Soon after leaving the chieftain she said they had difficulty finding drinking water. "*I was completely parched with thirst. Several hours past and still no sign of water; at last, I observed a beautiful lake shining in the distance; to describe to you the joy I felt is impossible, no words of mine can give an adequate idea of my feelings*".

Unfortunately, the "*beautiful lake*" turned out to be a

Starting to cross the desert

mirage.Not long after they came upon a camel train which had left Kapal, far to the south, to collect salt. But they had no water and were themselves looking for somewhere they could find some.

Thomas and Lucy's party then changed direction and then another disaster almost occurred when Lucy's horse bolted and she only avoided a nasty fall by grabbing the mane and holding fast to the reins. Another lake turned out to be saline. Women in a nearby yurt brought her milk and later mutton. They set off eastwards, in the direction of Lake Alakool, where they were assured they would find good water, but once again, on reaching the next aoul the water turned out to be little more than a stagnant pool.

Lucy says that after leaving here their path was over marshy ground with tall reeds and bulrushes, followed by very high grass and swampy soil. At times they were up to the saddle-flaps in mud and water and then had to deal with a camel which lay down and refused to get up. Although they are not precise on the location, it sounds very much like Lake Sassykol, the large lake to the west of Alakool, which has miles of reeds and bogs on its border.

By the 13th September Thomas and Lucy could see for the first time the snowy peaks of the Alatau Mountains far to the south. "I*t is a day I shall never forget*", wrote Lucy in *Recollections…* – and for good reason. They set off at 7 in the morning. Their Cossack Peter told them the ride would be 40 versts, although Alexae, the second Cossack, said it would be double that distance until they reached a place with good water. Both were wrong by a good margin.

By 4pm that afternoon it was clear that they were no closer to their destination and so they began to eat the melon Lucy had been given in Ayaguz. For Lucy, this was the first time she had ever tasted melon and she says "*It appeared to me the most delicious thing I had ever tasted in my life*". But still the journey went on, verst after verst.

None of the Cossacks appeared to know where they were and even the Kazakhs could only point towards the distant mountains. Thomas thought they were another 40 or 50 versts. As the sun began to sink, they kept on going, searching for any sign of habitation.

By 2am the following morning, there was still no aoul in sight and things were getting desperate. Lucy, by now freezing and exhausted, could scarcely hold the reins of her horse, having only a dress on. Her warm jacket had fallen from her horse earlier and not been noticed as missing until it was too late to go back. She lay down on a bearskin whilst Thomas put his fur-lined *tshube* over her. He also gave her a glass of rum. After 30 minutes or so she began to revive. One of the Cossacks now said they must remount, otherwise they would all be lost. The horses would not go forward after the sun rose unless they first got to water.

With the *tshube* tied over her, Lucy managed to move on for another two hours before once again dismounting and beginning to walk. Thomas persuaded her to get back on the horse again for another hour. Again she tried to dismount, telling Thomas to go on and bring water back for her. "*My husband now held me by the hand, in the other I kept the reins, but that was all, I had no power to guide my poor horse.*" In his diary, which appears to be the source of Lucy's account of the whole saga, Thomas says that Lucy told him to let her die there on the steppe. "*I now began to fear she would sink under this fatigue,*" he wrote.

As the sun began to rise, and in order to encourage her, Thomas told Lucy he thought he had heard a dog bark, a sure sign of nearby human settlement. "*I told Lucy. She said I only fancied so or wished her to think so and go on, but she said it was impossible.*" She struggled on, but was now very weak. Soon after he heard the dogs again. "*No music ever sounded so sweet in my ears and when Lucy heard them she cheered up and we went on,*" Thomas wrote in his diary. "*At 5 o'clock we got to an aoul belonging to a mullah. He did all that he could for us. Tea was soon made which we drank with infinite delight, but Lucy could eat nothing.*"

Not long after they were joined by one of the Cossacks he had sent forward earlier in the night to try to find the aoul they had been searching for, but who had also missed it. They eventually found it a few hours later and decided to halt there for the day to recover from what must have been a terrible ordeal, particularly for the heavily pregnant Lucy. Later that day Thomas reflected on the journey, which had totalled around 150 versts, sustained only by water-melon and a tot of rum:

> "*The Cossacks were wrong in not ascertaining if water could be procured on our route, as the want of this*

Thomas Atkinson's drawing of Kazakh tombs on the route south towards Kapal

when riding over the hot sand was severely felt by both of us – in August a party of Cossacks on their march to Kapal had crossed this part of the steppe. Several had died on the road. We saw their graves. These caused sad reflections as it might have been our case. We should (never) have been put into the sand without anyone knowing who or what we were."

Despite not mentioning this event in any of his public writings, in his diary Thomas is highly respectful of Lucy:

"I can't speak too highly of Lucy's courage and endurance during 22 hours on horseback, frequently riding very fast in the day and then riding through the nights across such a desert. Here we might have been plundered and overpowered had some of the bands of Baruntu[2] known of our march. Our arms were all kept in readiness and several would have bit the dust ere we had been taken. The part we rode over in the night

was a most singular place. There must have been thousands of the conical mounds. Frequently we crossed them and at other times rode round their bases. I should like much to see this place in the daylight – still I have no wish for another such a ride under the same circumstances."[3]

What is most remarkable about the story of Lucy's brush with death is its omission from Thomas' book, *Travels in the Regions of the Upper and Lower Amoor,* which contains the description of his and Lucy's journey to Kapal in 1848. Despite the drama, Thomas could not include it because of his fear that his bigamy would be discovered. There is little doubt that his book would have been even more dramatic than it was already, but all references to Lucy had to be resisted. Ironically, the absence of any mention of Lucy – or indeed of his son Alatau – in either of his books has led some critics to believe that Thomas was callous or egotistical. But his diary entries, which seldom fail to mention Lucy and which, time after time, show his deep love and affection for his very brave wife, prove that this was not the case.

Even now they had reached a resting place with fresh water, the journey was not over. It was a further two days on horseback until they could reach the banks of the Lepsou River – a journey over rolling low hills and deep sand in which the horses often sank up to their knees.

The camels were left far behind, but after six hours they began to make firmer ground. Both Thomas and Lucy mention the large numbers of *kurgans* (barrows) scattered across the steppe, as well as straight canals, some still containing running water and which dated back many hundreds of years.

By Thursday 16th September the Alatau Mountains were now plainly in view, their snowy peaks catching the early morning sun. They were riding parallel to the mountains at a distance Thomas calculated as 100 versts. The strong wind from the mountains whipped up the sand around them, creating dust devils: *"We saw several times during our ride columns of sand carried up by the wind. Sometimes five and six were seen, each turning round its own axis and moving slowly over the steppe. They sometimes rose to a great elevation. When seen with the sun shining upon them they appeared like pillars of smoke. But when seen looking towards the sun they were dark whirling masses. I was anxious to get to them but never succeeded. They were often from six to ten versts distant."*[4] As they came within sight of the Lepsou Lucy gave her horse free rein and galloped towards the banks. *"I drank freely of it and I thought it the sweetest water I had ever tasted in my life,"* she wrote.

They now rode south-west, parallel to the Alatau Mountain chain, but still on the grassy flat lands that stretched way out into the desert towards Lake Balkhash. They crossed the river Bean and noted the large number of *kurgans* and extensive earthworks in the area.

One, located on the Lepsou, Thomas describes as a parallelogram *"about 700 yards in length and 300 in breadth. The earth walls are now about 12 feet high and have been considerably higher; their thickness is about 16 feet at the bottom and nine feet at the top. This enclosure was entered by four gates, one being in the centre of each side; but the eastern end has been partly destroyed by the river which is gradually cutting down the bank."*

Thomas and Lucy were now entering the Zhetysu, known in Russian as Semirechye – or Seven Rivers region.[5] These rivers, which all flow into or towards Lake Balkhash, originate in the glaciers and lakes of the Alatau Mountains. Bounded by Lake Alakool to the north-east, Balkash to the north and west and the Alatau Mountains to the south, much of the Zhetysu region, with the exception of the river valleys, is dry and inhospitable.

During the Atkinsons' time the tribes of the Great and Middle Hordes would spend the summers with their huge herds of animals in the *jailau* (alpine meadows) of the Alatau Mountains and would migrate to the shores of Lake Balkash in the autumn, where they would settle in for the winter.

The Atkinsons' route from the banks of the Lepsou to Kapal is not clear from either of their accounts. Thomas refers to a group of mountains in front of the Djungarian Alatau as the Karatau. This name no longer exists, but there is a group of hills that sits to the south-west of Lake Alakool, which fits their description. Between this small range, which lies to the south of the modern town of Usharal, and the Djungar Alatau there is a wide valley, which Thomas describes entering after crossing the mountains.

He describes a hard journey where they could only ride single file and where eventually they had to dismount and lead their animals up a narrow ravine towards the top, from which they got a very clear view of the Alatau chain, with its snowy peaks.

Thomas knew the Russians were building a fort somewhere on the River Kapal, but was not sure of the exact location. He kept moving towards the main Alatau chain, noting the Acsou and Sarcand Rivers. It seems likely that his group made their way up what is today known as the Hasford Pass, from where far below him he would have been able to see the gorge from which the Acsou River pours out of the mountains.

The entry to the pass today is just outside Zhansugurov, which was once called Abakumovka after the Cossack commanding officer at Kapal. From its highest point you can see the villages of Suyuksai and Arasan, which are on the old Cossack post road that once linked Kapal (and later, Almaty) with Ayuguz. Thomas says that on the 20th September, just at dusk, they reached a group of yurts, *"to the great astonishment of the*

The old Cossack road running along the base of the Djungar Alatau Mountains

Cossack inhabitants." This was the new settlement of Kapal. The officers, who explained that their expedition had arrived a month previously, welcomed the Atkinsons, who spent the rest of the evening giving them the latest news from Europe.

In the morning Thomas found some of the Cossacks, of whom there were around 500, busy throwing up the earthworks for a V-Shaped military bastion facing out into the Steppes. Others were preparing timbers to make log cabins. He tells us that the first Cossacks had arrived in the region four years previously and had built an artillery platform at the mouth of the gorge from which the River Kapal sprang from the mountains. In those days it had taken 42 days of route-marching to reach the camp, although this had been reduced to 18 days by the time Thomas and Lucy arrived.

The impending arrival of winter meant there was an added urgency to the work of the Cossacks. Many had brought their wives and children with them and now they had to make shelters. They used whatever was available, taking stones from the river gorge to build the walls and making roofs from tree trunks covered with nine inches of earth. Instead of window glass, they used Chinese silk, strained onto frames.

In August 2014 I saw the original Cossack bastion at Kapal for the first time. Its V-shape is still clearly visible, as are the large ditches in front of it. There is still some trace of the buildings that were once within the bastion and even the most cursory inspection turns up artefacts that date from the 19th century. We found old hand-sewn leather boots and plenty of brass cartridge shells –

Remains of the V-shaped Cossack bastion in Kapal

although the latter probably dated from the early 20th century. For several years, until the establishment of Vierney (Almaty) in 1854, this was the most important military outpost in the Kazakh Steppe and even then, one of the remotest points in the Russian Empire. It was to be home for Thomas and Lucy for the following eight months.

By the time they reached Kapal, Thomas and Lucy had already travelled very substantial distances. Lucy calculated it thus:

> "*Since I left you in February last, I have travelled in a carriage 6,267 versts, on horseback 2,040, in boats and on a raft 760. This is the distance we have gone in the direct road; but I have done much more, having been on several excursions on horseback; for instance, the very evening after our arrival here, we went on a trip of 17 versts. This year my husband has travelled 10,705 versts in a carriage, 2,290 on horseback, and 1,490 in boats, exclusive of divers excursions for sketching of 40 or 50 versts distance; so, you see, the ground we have gone over is immense: –*

	Versts.	English miles
My husband in all direct travelling	14,485	About 10,864
I the same	9,067	about 6,800

Despite the prospect of a further ride north of well over 1,000 kilometres, it seems that the original intention of Thomas and Lucy had been to return to Barnaul in the Altai before the winter set in. However, their plans were disrupted by two major events. The first was a weather event. Well before the end of October, winter began to arrive with a vengeance. Snow began to cover the shelters the Cossacks had been digging into the earth.

By November the *bourans* – harsh, Siberian winds laden with snow – began to blow off the steppes, sometimes lasting for days at a time, "*during which,*" wrote Thomas, "*men could not proceed twenty paces from their dwellings.*" On the morning of the 23rd November a huge gale began which soon transformed into a hurricane, "*sweeping the snow into clouds like flour, rendering it almost dark at midday.*"

Overnight the weather deteriorated and the Cossack commander, Captain Abakumov told Thomas that it would

Dust devils in the desert

get even worse. Already the primitive huts in which most of the soldiers were living were covered by deep snow. As soon as passages were cleared, they were filled again.

"At length each party became prisoners in their dwellings, from which they could not proceed five paces. They had now great difficulty in cooking; and those most distant from the kitchen found it a constant labour to keep up a communication with *that necessary establishment. When the snow became deep enough, a gallery was formed in it and then they passed to and fro without difficulty."[6]*

The bouran lasted until the 4th December – 11 days in all. It must have been all the more terrifying for Lucy because barely a month before, on 4 November, she had given birth, two months prematurely, to a baby boy.   ∎

1   Recollections, op cit, p58

2   Thomas' usage is slightly wrong here. A *bouran* is a raid carried out by mounted Kazakh horsemen, usually on the aoul of a rival, and in order to steal animals – and sometimes women and children. His use of the term 'bit the dust' is a very early usage of this phrase, more usually associated with Westerns.

3   1848 diary, entry for 14 September 1848.

4   1848 diary, entry for 16 September 1848

5   The seven rivers traditionally associated with the Zhetysu are: the Ili, the Karatal, the Bean, the Acsou, the Sarcan, the Bascan and the Lepsou.

6   Amoor, op cit, p94.

Thomas Atkinson discussing the journey to Lake Zaisan with two Kazakhs wearing horse-skin coats

Chapter
SEVEN

LIFE IN KAPAL

According to a story told to Thomas, not a great deal of thought had gone into the siting of Kapal. Referrring to events that had taken place in the early 1840s, he writes:

"A brace of generals, with a numerous staff, were sent into the steppe to determine upon the site of the new fort," he writes. *"Stores and creature comforts of all kinds accompanied the two heroes, among which champagne was a prominent item. A strong guard of Cossacks formed their escort and numerous cooks and bakers were also attached to the expedition. A party of Cossacks and cooks were always sent on in advance to select the place for encampment and to prepare a sumptuous entertainment and strict orders were given that the day's march should not be a long one."*

Thomas says that after reaching the easternmost valley of the Lepsou River, a beautiful spot now near the town of Lepsinsk, the generals and their entourage decided to stop for a few days. From here they moved on to the river Kapal, more than 600 kilometres south of Semipalatinsk, but found it so desolate that they decided to halt at this point and order the construction of a fort. With that, says Thomas, the generals returned to the north.

Soon after this, in the summer of 1846, an advance party of 70 Cossacks and 80 artillerymen arrived under the command of Cossack Captain Nukhalov and built a gun emplacement in the mouth of the gorge out of which the River Kapal burst from the Alatau Mountains. When the main body of Cossacks arrived in late August 1848 under the overall command of the regular Imperial army officer, Captain Abakumov, they started building a V-shaped bastion about 400 metres from the river,

A view in the Kora Valley, close to Kapal

Nick Fielding

The entrance to the Tamchiboulac Spring in Kapal

on rising ground. At that time, says Thomas, "*not a single tree was visible and scarcely a bush could be found, except on the banks of the river, and even there they were few.*" Kapal was one of four Cossack pickets founded in the region, the others being Kargaly, Topalevsk and Arasan. The defended villages acted as post-stations for the regular military despatches that were sent up the line to Russia every Monday. In total there were 12 pickets between Ayaguz and Kapal, each with two pairs of horses.

The first problem encountered at Kapal by Mr Loganov, the Cossack engineer officer, was the lack of nearby timber. The nearest source was more than 20 miles away, close to the gorge of the Acsou River, from where it had to be cut down and transported by bullocks back to the fort. First to be built were the fort, the storehouses and the hospital. Only then could the individual Cossacks begin work on the hovels in which they would have to live that first winter with their women and children. Thomas says most of these rooms were

12 feet square, in which two families totalling up to 10 people, would have to live. Many simply dug pits, which they covered with branches and earth.

At first Thomas and the heavily pregnant Lucy were given a yurt in which to stay. After a few weeks, the garrison commander obviously took pity on Lucy and just before Alatau was born, they moved into a two-roomed house. "*I now often think what would have become of me had we been in a yurt when I was confined. I believe both I and the child must have died,*" she wrote.

Life was not entirely grim at Kapal. Lucy notes that at the end of September and beginning of October she and Thomas would take long rides around Kapal and in the evenings would assemble with Baron George Gotthard Moritz Ernst Wrangel, a Livonian (German-Baltic) army officer in the Tsar's service who was district commander and whose yurt was next to that of the Atkinsons. From the 18th January 1848 Baron Wrangel was appointed officer in charge of the Great Kazakh Horde. Lucy gives a wonderful description of her first meeting with the baron, who had received a sabre wound whilst fighting in the Caucasus and still bore the scar:

> "*Baron Wrangel, the governor, was much surprised at seeing a lady enter, and perhaps also at my appearance, for, to say truth, I was not very presentable. On our journey I had mounted camels and bulls as well as horses, but the last day, having a stream to cross to enable me to reach a Tartar encampment, I found it too deep to ford pleasantly, as the water would reach to my waist. Whilst hesitating what was best to be done, a Kazakh, who had followed us down the bank, without ceremony walked into the water, and, placing himself before me in a stooping posture, patted his back, and signed for me to mount, which I at last did, and crossed on the man's back.*
> "*We found the Baron sitting cross-legged on a stool, with a long Turkish pipe in his mouth, a small Tartar cap on his head, and a dressing-gown, à la Kazakh. Mr. Loganov, the engineering officer, and the topographer, were dressed in exactly the same way. They all gave us a most cordial welcome: we sat chatting till a late hour. The tent in which we found the party assembled was very large, and used as the common sitting-room; each had a small one for a sleeping apartment, one was allotted to us, and*

another was used as a kitchen: thus we formed quite a little colony."[1]

So the other officers were: Captain Abakumov and Captain Loganov, the engineer; Captain Izmaelov, the commander of the Cossacks; Captain Tochinskoi, his second-in-command; two young lieutenants, one of whom was a surgeon. There was also a topographer and a store-keeper.

Food in Kapal was basic: no vegetables at all, no butter or eggs. Mostly they ate meat and rice, with coarse, black bread, which "even Mr Atkinson had some difficulty swallowing". Lucy did not drink the brick tea that was usually on offer in Kazakh yurts, although Thomas usually did so, if only so as not to hurt the feelings of his host.

Despite the lack of culinary choice, it appears to have been a jolly place. In the evenings the officers would gather together to be entertained by Baron Wrangel's inexhaustible fund of entertaining anecdotes. He would accompany Thomas' flute-playing on the guitar and evenings would often end with the singing of the Russian and English national anthems.

On at least one occasion, there was a grand ball to celebrate the arrival of some of the officers' wives from Semipalatinsk. Lucy gives a wonderful description of her preparations for the ball: "*Having but one dress besides my travelling one, I drew it forth and looked with dismay at its tumbled appearance. I had a small iron with me fortunately, the only one in Kapal, so I despatched our Cossack to and fro to the kitchen to have it heated. Thus, with a flannel petticoat for an ironing blanket, and a box for a table, I managed to make it decent, and forthwith I commenced my toilet. The guests were bidden for five o'clock, but our host begged of me to be ready earlier to receive his lady visitors. In the midst of my dressing a bouran arose; I was obliged to rush to one side of the tent to hold it down, my candle was blown out, leaving me in total darkness. Mr. Atkinson ran outside to call the men, who were heard screaming and running in all directions, as the kitchen, with all the delicacies for the coming feast, was being nearly swept away; at last, with ropes and beams of wood, it, as well as our tent, was secured. With some difficulty I got a light, and resumed my dressing; in the meantime, I received three notes to hasten operations.*"

As soon as she was ready, Lucy entered the main house where the ball was to be held. She found the Baron in full uniform,

but the grandest man in the room was his Kazakh bodyguard, Yarolae: "*He wore a magnificent new dressing-gown, a splendid shawl round his waist, and a tall-pointed silk cap, and red boots; altogether he looked and felt superb.*" All around the room were newly constructed stools, with a carpet-covered dias at one end. Here Lucy, as hostess, took her position, whilst Yarolae announced the entry of the first ladies:

> "*Walking like a prince into the centre of the apartment, he announced, in a voice like thunder, 'Madame Ismaeloff and Madame Tetchinskoy.' The contrast between them and the gaily-attired Kazakh was too striking. The former lady was a sorry-faced old body, with a bright shining skin, a clean dark-coloured cotton dress, a white collar which reached to her shoulders, a white cap with a very full border, a lilac silk shawl, and brown worsted gloves, completed her attire; her companion, a small person, had a similar dress, but instead of the shawl she wore a pink satin mantle, trimmed with white lace.*
> "*They came up to me, each giving me three kisses, and took a seat on either side of me, without uttering a word. Yarolae was again off; the next visitor was proclaimed by the roaring of a bull. The door was thrown open very wide, and 'Anna Pavlovna' was announced. My gravity was this time sorely tried, and more so as I glanced at the Baron; his face was irresistible, he went forward to shake Anna by the hand; her deep-toned sonorous voice resounded through the room.*"

This lady was a tall and rather stout woman, dressed in a Russian *sarafan* (peasants' dress) a coloured cotton shawl, shoes but no stockings. A bright red cloth was bound round her head. "*As you may imagine, she was gloveless, but what an arm and hand she had! Big enough to knock down anyone who approached her ungraciously.*"

The final two ladies were from Bisk in the Altai and, says Lucy, "*had more pretensions than the others.*"

> "*Madame Serabrikoff had on a woollen dress, and the other a faded green silk, with a patch in the skirt, of another colour; this latter visitor found means during the evening of telling me that she had not expected the ball to take place so soon, otherwise she would have had her polka ready to wear; it was a beautiful blue satin, which had been presented to her on leaving Bisk.*"

Thomas Atkinson's drawing of the Tombs of the Genii in the Kora Valley

To begin with the Russian ladies sat bolt upright, trying to look stately, until they had had a drink or two, when there was an almost immediate transformation. Lucy reproached the Baron for offering Chinese spirit, but he told her that they all expected it and would not be happy if no drink had been offered.

As for Thomas, he spent his days sketching the scenery around Kapal or out in the mountains, exploring the remote valleys and ridges to the south of the town. On fine days Thomas was able to get out on horseback and hunt with Captain Abakumov or some of the other officers. He describes setting off south with a party of 17 on one occasion to cross the Myn-Chukur ridge behind Kapal and cross into the valley of the Kora River. Even today this is a very difficult journey, but at that time, it must have been very dangerous indeed. But it is worth it for the scenery alone. On reaching the top of the ridge, Thomas described the view below:

"*As we stood looking into the depth, probably 5,000 feet below us, the river appeared like a band of frosted silver; we could also hear the roaring of the water as it rushed over its rocky bed… This side of the valley was exceedingly abrupt; indeed, in many parts the precipices were perpendicular; in other places the declivity was so steep that neither man nor horse could maintain a footing, nor were there either trees or bushes growing on any part. The opposite side, facing the north, was well wooded, the trees extending from the bank of the river upwards, till they diminished at the snow line.*"[2]

Thomas was deeply struck by the beauty of the Kora Valley, as he devotes almost two chapters to describing it and to telling the folklore associated with it. One particular mystery concerns the five massive stones he describes in the valley standing on their ends. One, he says, was 76 feet high, while the others were from 45 to 50 feet high. Close by was a massive pile of stones, 28 feet high and 42 feet in diameter and which appeared to be a huge tomb.

According to one of his Kazakh guides, the Kora Valley (the name itself means 'sealed' valley), was once the home of powerful genii, who constantly feuded with other geniis in the Tarbagatai region. There followed a huge battle between the rivals, which was only settled when Shaitan himself made an appearance and crushed the geniis, burying them beneath these huge stones. Hence the meaning of the name.

I spent several days trying to locate these standing stones, but could not find them, although there are other massive stones in the valley. One local source said that there had been many landslides and earthquakes in the region and that it was likely the original stones had long since been toppled over and broken up. Perhaps this is true, or perhaps they remain to be discovered?

Thomas travelled extensively in the Kora Valley, visiting all the side valleys, lakes and glaciers, sketching whenever he could. The entire valley is about 90 kilometres in length. At its western end is the industrial city of Tekeli, but no entry can be gained there because of the valley's steep sides. At the other end, are the great Tronov, Bezsonov and Sapozhnikov glaciers.

Thomas was certainly very happy travelling through this valley, noting on the 4th October, for example, that he had experienced "*one of the most lovely mornings I had ever beheld.*" The following day he awoke to find very different conditions, with more than a foot of snow, which was continuing to fall. It was time to leave. A great storm rolled in and it took the group three days to get out of the valley.

From the top, looking to the north, the steppes looked peaceful and Kapal was still basking in the last vestiges of autumn warmth. But they had been lucky and they knew it. Undeterred, Thomas and a smaller party set off shortly after to visit the valley of the River Bean, about 20 miles to the east, where he had been told of the existence of a huge cavern.

Thomas also spent time in Kapal working at his paintings. He notes that his first work was a large watercolour, which soon after he sent to Prince Gortchakov by courier, as he had promised to do. "*While dabbling in my colour-box, discomfort and even hunger were forgotten and the occupation enabled me to smile at the disasters of a stormy winter and to enjoy the amusements of my companions*", he wrote.

Chief of whom, of course, was Lucy. Soon enough the day of Lucy's confinement approached. She makes light of the circumstances surrounding the birth of her baby boy. In *Recollections…* she teases her anonymous correspondent about why she had not written:

"*But you are already asking what excuse I can make for the two last weeks. Here I have a little family history to*

A woodcut of a glacier in the Kora Valley

relate. You must understand that I was in expectation of a little stranger, whom I thought might arrive about the end of December or the beginning of January."

By these calculations, Lucy had become pregnant only weeks after setting off with Thomas from Moscow, following their wedding in February. That must have seemed like a lifetime ago. Since then she had travelled thousands of miles by carriage, horse, camel and even on the backs of bulls. She says she had hoped to be back in Barnaul for the birth and therefore had not prepared for the event,

"When lo and behold! On the 4th November, at twenty minutes past four pm, he made his appearance. The young doctor here said he would not live more than seven days, but, thank Heaven, he is still alive and well. He is small, but very much improved since his birth. I shall let him get a little bigger before I describe him. He is to be called Alatau, as he was born at the foot of this mountain range; and his second name Tamchiboulac, this being a dropping-spring, close to which he was called into existence."

Glaciers on the south side of the Kora Valley

Nick Fielding

The young military surgeon told Lucy the premature birth was due to *"excessive exercise on horseback"*, surely one of the great understatements of all time. She added that no-one should have any illusions about the doctor: *"Doubtless, seeing I speak of the doctor, you imagine we have a competent one here. Far from it, he is but twenty-three years of age; theoretically he may be clever, practically certainly not. When my husband applied to him in my case, he declared he had not the slightest knowledge of anything of the kind."*

Lucy says that it was fortunate that Thomas was at home, as he had returned only the evening before, having been absent two days on a shooting expedition. However, it is unclear that he attended the birth himself – very unlikely during those days. She says she does not know what she would have done without the help of Madame Tetchinskoy, one of the recently-arrived officers' wives, during what must have been a terrifying night following the birth:

"During the night the bouran was so terrific that not a sound scarcely could be heard within doors. I never closed my eyes during that night; my heart was lifted up in thankfulness to the Creator for all His mercies to me.

Had this event occurred one short week earlier, and on such a night, what should I have done? The child was enveloped in furs and placed on a leathern trunk against the stove to keep him warm; the woman was stretched on the floor wrapped in a sheep-skin. I lay on my bed, hearing the poor infant, when there was a moment's lull in the storm, moaning. I screamed to the woman to give the poor little thing to me, but not a sound did she hear; at last, after about two hours I managed to awaken her, and make her understand; she took up the poor babe, and poking it at me like a bundle of straw, down she was again immediately; the instant the child touched me, it ceased its moaning. They had placed in its mouth a piece of muslin, containing black bread and sugar dipped in water, and, indeed, this was all he had till the third day, when he received his natural food."

It turned out that Madame Tetchinskoy was not quite as respectable as her married position suggested. In fact, she had previously been condemned to receive a hundred lashes for *"destroying her infant ere it saw the light"* and, wrote Lucy, *"probably at this moment she would not have been alive had not a Cossack*

A woodcut showing Kapal before the onset of winter

come forward and offered to marry her before she had undergone the sentence, and he received fifteen lashes instead of her – such is the law. They are living very happily together: to judge from all I have seen, she is a very kind woman, willing to oblige when she can."

Alatau's birth was a major event in Kapal. Other children had been born that month, but not one survived; others who had been born on the journey across the steppe all died. Alatau was the only one who lived. In the old Cossack cemetery in Kapal you can still find some of the gravestones put up at that time to commemorate the many people who died during the early years of the town.

That winter more than 100 people died and Thomas described the pitiable scenes:

"It was truly heart-rending to look upon their miserable families when the storms were raging; some were seen

trying to shelter themselves under strips of voilock and others were lying down to sleep in corners of half-roofed rooms…First the children sank under this severity and were carried in numbers to the graves; the poor miserable mothers, worn out by anxiety, fatigue and bad food, next fell victims to the fatal maladies which assailed them. I have often watched the mournful processions wending their way to the hill selected for the cemetery, about two miles distant from the fort and when they have passed have turned away with gloomy foreboding for the future. The endurance of the Cossacks lasted a little longer, but their turn was approaching."

Having seen all the gravestones at the old cemetery in Kapal, I began to wonder where they had come from. They are not typical Orthodox grave markers, but many are long, thin stones over two metres in length. The mystery was solved by my good friend and translator Vladimir Gostyevski, who lives in the nearby town of Tekeli. Vladimir noticed one of Thomas's drawings of Kapal showing a large *kurgan* (barrow) at a distance. The *kurgan* is still there, but something is missing. When Thomas drew the *kurgan* it was surrounded by large, long, thin stones, doubtless placed there in antiquity. Now they are absent. Could these be the same stones, with writing crudely carved by a mason in the camp during those dreadful early years? I have little doubt that this is the case.

And what about the name of the child? Alatau Tamchiboulac Atkinson is surely one of the most distinctive names ever carried by an Englishman. We cannot be sure how Thomas and Lucy decided on the names, but they were passed down within the family for several generations. It was a brave decision to give such names to the child, but they were carried with pride by their bearer throughout his eventful life. He too had an adventurous life and in 1869 migrated from England to Hawaii, where he became director of education, editor of the *Hawaiian Gazette* and was eventually responsible for organising the first census of the islands. He died in 1906.

Today, the Tamchiboulac Spring at Kapal is still famous throughout the district. People come from all around to fill bottles with the water which, they say, contains all the naturally occurring elements in the periodic table. At any time of day you will find people there, in the deep glade where water pours from the rocks in front of you. It has clearly been in use for hundreds, if not thousands, of years, a place where clean, life-giving water could be found.

Some people say that even the name of the town, Kapal, is linked directly to the spring. They say that in Russian, the sound of water dropping to the floor is written onomatopoeically as '*kapali-kapali-kapali*' and that this is the origin of the name. Others link it to the name of a famous *batyr* (warrior) prince, but this question has never been finally resolved. Close by, at Arasan, is another spring whose waters are famous throughout Kazakhstan for their healing powers. Both springs source their water from the Djungar Alatau.

Lucy got up for the first time the day after Alatau was born, walking about the room for a few minutes. The following day she was up after breakfast and stayed up the whole day. And from then on she was up every day.

Lucy says that all the women at Kapal advised her to swaddle

Nick Fielding

Gravestone from the Old Cossack cemetery at Kapal. Were they taken from local kurgans?

Thomas Atkinson's drawing of kurgans at Kapal surrounded by tall stones

Alatau, as was customary with Russian children at the time. But the child would not allow it and the project was abandoned. She says that he only awoke at bathing time and for another hour or so a day for the first month of his life. *"Even the second month I scarcely had him in my arms, and, until he was nine months old, he never had a tear in his eyes. I have seen him restless and uneasy, and it was very remarkable that this always took place before a storm: he was as good as a barometer on the road."*

There was one other incident in Kapal that Thomas certainly had good cause to remember. It happened during the Christmas holidays, when Captain Abakumov suggested that he and Thomas should take an evening drive in his sledge. The 'sledge', it turned out, was little more than a wicker basket on runners with straw in the bottom covered by wolf skins. This unusual contraption was to be drawn by three fierce Kazakh stallions. Thomas stepped in, but before Abakumov could get in, the horses bolted, throwing the yemtschick from his seat. Thomas describes his terrifying experience: *"They dashed off at full speed, going straight towards the ravine. I understood my position in an instant – to attempt to leap from the sledge would have been certain death and I decided to take my chance in the gorge, believing this to be the least dangerous. The horses rushed madly on and I felt that a few minutes would decide the fate of all of us, the ravine being sixty feet deep at this par*t.*"*

Alatau Tamchiboulac Atkinson 1848-1906

Just short of the ravine, the horses turned, throwing the sledge almost over the edge. They raced away, increasing in speed, with the basket almost turning over and trapping Thomas' hand at one point. It was not until almost five miles from the fort that one of the horses fell and the other two drew to a halt. Soon there were artillerymen everywhere, gripping the reins and helping Thomas from the basket. He realised that he had broken a finger and had a long chip of wood driven far up beneath one of his nails that he drew out with pliers, and Captain Abakumov set the broken finger with splints. The next day, says Thomas, he was unable to stand, but following a sauna he felt much better. It was several weeks before the finger bone healed.

With the coming of spring, political developments in the steppe were beginning to take shape. The Kazakh tribes in this part of Semirechye had been split over whether or not to accept Russian rule. In 1847 the revolt led by Kenisary Kasimov had come to an end with his capture

and decapitation by one of the Kyrgyz tribes. The arrival of the Russians and the establishment of their forts along the border with China clearly had a substantial effect on the tribes and most now were in favour of accepting Russian rule, not least to protect them from the depredations of the Khans of Khokand and Bokhara, who regularly raided into their territories, seizing livestock, women and children.

In March 1849 a large gathering was held in Kapal, bringing together the leaders of the Great and Middle Hordes to discuss the boundary between their tribes. Senior Russian officials arrived from Ayaguz and Captain Abakumov was encouraged to put on an artillery display, not least to show the truculent tribes what to expect if they failed to accept Russian rule. It was witnessed by Thomas:

"During this operation many of the Kazakhs rushed forward to get a better view. Before they had gone half

Thomas Atkinson's
watercolour of the
Tamchiboulac Spring

Nick Fielding

The Tamchiboulac Spring in Kapal

*the distance the first gun belched forth its flame, smoke
and thunder, instantly checking their ardour and causing
a rapid retreat. As one gun after another echoed in the
mountains, they gazed with perfect horror and were
evidently greatly relieved when the salute was ended." [4]*

Sultan Souk, as one of the most senior leaders of the Great
Horde, was prominent in the proceedings. He listened as the
Russian officials explained that Prince Gortchikoff wished for
the two hordes to accept a boundary and to stop their mutual
raids. Sultan Souk said he would consent to a boundary
along the line of the Acsou River, a position supported by his
followers. In response, one of the officials said the boundary
should be along the line of the River Bean and that the Prince
would not consent to any other boundary. A chief from the
Middle Horde now spoke out in favour of the River Bean as
a boundary. Thus it was stalemate and despite several more
days of discussion, that is how things ended.

Souk was clearly a great favourite of Thomas and Lucy and they
learned much about his background. In his first book, Thomas
is rather dismissive of Souk and portrays him as vain, asking
Thomas not to draw his crooked nose. In the frontispiece of the
book he shows him wearing a gold medal presented to him by
Tsar Alexander I, but implies he had sold his birthright to gain
such a bauble. But by the second book, he is more sympathetic
and Lucy certainly has been won over. In fact, Thomas devotes
two whole chapters to the story of Souk's tragic elopement with
a Kyrgyz princess. Thomas starts the story with the history of

Souk's father, Sultan Timour, who at the beginning of the 19th
century was head of the Great Horde. A direct descendant of
Genghis Khan, his territory included almost all of what is today
known as Djungaria or Semirechye. To the south, the ruler in
the territory that is now Kyrgyzstan, was Sultan Djan-gir Khan.
Sultan Timour and Djan-gir Khan lived in uneasy proximity
to each other, sometimes uniting for raids, at other times at
loggerheads following a depredation by one group or the other.

As Sultan Timour's eldest son, Sultan Souk established a
reputation as a brave fighter whilst still in his early 20s and
it was clear that one day he would inherit his father's mantle
as chief of the Great Horde. When he indicated that he would
like to marry one of Djan-gir Khan's daughters, his father did
not object and sent messengers to the latter to conclude an
agreement. The Khan gave his consent to the marriage and all
that remained to be settled was the *kalym* – the bride price
paid by the groom's family. Thomas' story follows the exploits
of Sultan Souk as he attempts to visit his bride-to-be, in the
process outwitting and outrunning one of the many robber
bands that infested the region. After a dangerous journey of
almost 20 days he returned to his father's aoul, having met
his betrothed. Later that year, during winter when their aouls
were only three days apart from each other, Sultan Timour
decided to send another deputation to Djan-gir Khan to pay
the kalym.

The price demanded – 200 camels, 3,000 horses, 5,000 oxen
and 10,000 sheep – was thought too high by Sultan Timour's
retainers, who decided, reluctantly, to return empty-handed.
They had intended to offer about a third of what was being
asked and realised it would be seen as insulting even to make
the offer.

When Sultan Timour heard the price being demanded he was
enraged, saying it was an insult against his family and vowing
revenge. However, better counsel prevailed and the following
spring Souk decided to return back to the mountains to see Ai
Khanym, his intended wife, carrying with him a present and a
message to the Khan from his father. He was received warmly
enough, but Ai Khanym let Souk know that her father had
already promised her to the Khan of Badakhshan in northern
Afghanistan and that the marriage was scheduled for the
summer. She was not happy and told Souk she would happily
go wherever he chose to take her. He returned home to plan
his next step.

Thomas Atkinson has a narrow escape

Thomas Atkinson's painting of Sultan Souk and his family

The snowy peaks of the Djungar Alatau

Nick Fielding

The following May Souk returned again to the aoul of Djan-gir Khan, during which time he made arrangements with Ai Khanym, telling her he would return for her in June, before she was married off to the Afghan khan. He returned, only to run off with her into the mountains, travelling in the high pastures at the head of the Terek River, (itself the subject of a beautiful watercolour by Thomas, which now hangs in the dining room of the Royal Geographical Society in London) far to the east of the Lepsou and then down towards the Ili and the safety of the Great Horde. The story ended tragically for Souk. Despite eluding their pursuers, Souk's bride was killed by a tiger and the young man returned to his father's aoul empty-handed.

Time was now pressing on. Thomas and Lucy had left Moscow in February 1848 and had barely stayed beneath a conventional roof since then. Their child, lucky enough to survive a winter in which all the other newly-born children had died, was now nearly nine months old. Summer was

approaching fast and would offer the best chance of returning north to Barnaul in the Altai region of Siberia.

Thus it was that on 24th May 1849, after eight months in Kapal, Thomas, Lucy and Alatau set off back towards the north. They rode out past the Byan-ja-Rouk Mountain, across the steppe towards Arasan, accompanied by a large group of the Cossack officers on horseback and their wives in a *horse-drawn char-a-banc*.

At Arasan, famous even then for its thermal waters, there was singing, dancing and a feast before everyone turned in for the night. The following day it was only Captain Abakumov who travelled on further with them, over the Hasford Pass, together with their Cossack guides. From the top they could see the rivers Sarcand, Bascan and the Acsou far below them rushing onwards from the mountains towards distant Lake Balkash. That is where they would spend the next few months, exploring the remarkable river valleys in the Djungar Alatau. ◼

Thomas Atkinson's painting of the Terric-Sou in the Djungar Alatau

Royal Geographical Society – Institute of British Geographers

1. *Recollections*, p111
2. *Amoor*, op cit, p100
3. *Ibid*, p164-5
4. *Ibid*, p175

Chapter
EIGHT

EXPLORING THE DJUNGAR ALATAU

Soon after leaving their friends at Arasan on the 24th May 1848, Thomas and Lucy, together with their baby son Alatau, headed on horseback for the remote valley of the Acsou River, about 20 miles away across the vast steppe dotted with dozens of *kurgans* – signs that this area had been inhabited for thousands of years. The Acsou is one of the seven rivers of the Semirechye region and it appears that Thomas' aim was to visit as many of these beautiful river valleys as possible.[1] All flow out from the massive glaciers of the Djungar Alatau towards Lake Balkash across the steppe.

In fact, following the course of the Acsou into the mountains is almost impossible. In the summer of 2014, I tried myself to ascend the Acsou, but after a long hike was defeated as the mountains closed in and the path disappeared. The only way to get any higher towards the source is to climb the mountains flanking this very steep-sided gorge.

Somewhere in the mountains close to the source of the Bascan – there are Big and Little Bascan rivers – Lucy says that they saw a place that appeared to be a vast crater, surrounded by large masses of granite, with a cone-like shape in the centre. There were two circles of rocks around the centre of this place, which they dubbed Granite Crater. From this high point, Lucy says they saw a sunset over the steppe:

> *"The steppe was spread out like a map, the rivers looking like threads of silver, whilst towards the Balkash lay a boundless dreary waste, where at this time of the year it would be frightful to travel; then the golden tints of the sky I try in vain to find language to describe. Those who have not visited these regions can form no conception of the splendour of an evening scene over the steppe."*

High above the Bascan River are some of the biggest mountains in the Djungar Alatau. The gorge of the Little Baskan

River begins from just beneath the Zhambyl glacier, one of the largest glaciers in the region. The three highest peaks of the Djungar Alatau are on the eastern side of Zhambyl glacier: Semenov Tien-Shansky peak (4622m), Shumskoi (4442m) and the peak of Abay (4460m); Zhambyl peak (4249m) is found above the western part of Zhambyl glacier. The tallest peak, named after the Russian explorer Petr Petrovich Semenov Tien-Shansky, straddles the border between Kazakhstan and China. To the west of the peak is the Amanbokter pass (3933m) which leads from the Little Baskan gorge in Kazakhstan to valley of the Boro-Tala river in China.

From here above the Bascan Lucy says they decided to descend to the Lepsou River, down dangerous paths of almost impossible steepness. At every turn they saw Kazakhs in their high summer pastures with their animals. At one point, far below them, they spotted a lake of extraordinary green colour, which they tried to reach. Finding the way impossible, they retraced their tracks back to the Lepsou River via an easier route with the intention of heading back up the mountain to try and locate the lake they had glimpsed.

On 2nd June they reached Sarcand, where they pitched tent. They had to cross the river on a narrow, frail bridge made of little more than a few trees laid across the stream from a large stone in the centre. "*The crossing was not agreeable*", wrote Lucy, "*seeing the raging torrent under our horses' feet. One false step, and all would have been finished. The noise of the stones being brought down, and the roar of the torrent, was so deafening, that we were obliged to go close up to each other to hear a word that was spoken. At last it became really painful; the head appeared full to bursting. I walked away some distance to try and get a little relief, but it was useless; a verst from the river the roar was still painfully heard. This din, coupled with the thunder, was awful; the latter we had almost daily – indeed, when it did not take place, there seemed to be a want in our life – and in these stupendous mountain masses it was fearfully grand, there being a short heavy growl in the distance, as if the spirits of the storm were crushing huge mountains together, and grinding them to powder; and the lightning descended in thick streams.*"[2]

Thomas Atkinson's watercolour of the Acsou River gorge in the Djungar Alatau

From Sarcand, where they spent a few days exploring the area, on 8th June they headed back into the mountains. As they advanced up the river valley, they met many of the Kazakhs they had first seen a year before when travelling across the steppes. These large groups had been travelling from their winter quarters on Lake Balkash for the previous two months, on the way to their summer pastures – *jailau* – in the Djungar Alatau Mountains.

Many of them were charmed by the baby Alatau, often asking if they could keep him. Some even argued that Alatau belonged to them, as he was born in their territory, had been fed by their sheep and other animals, ridden their horses and received their name. Leave him with us, they said, and he will become a great chief. They brought him presents, including pieces of silk, ikats from Bokhara, young lambs and goats to ride upon. One sultan told Lucy that if she would leave him he would be given a stud of horses and attendants.

Lucy says that some of the tribes had never seen a European woman, with the strangest of consequences:

"*These believed I was not a woman, and that, I being a man, we were curiosities of nature; that Allah was to be praised for his wonderful works – two men to have a baby! One of our Cossacks I thought would have dropped from his horse with laughter. I was obliged to doff my hat, unfasten my hair, and let it stream around me, to try and convince them; but this did not at first satisfy them, still I believe at last I left them under a conviction that I was not the wonderful being they had first imagined me to be. My stays were objects of much speculation; they imagined they were never taken off. When told they were usually worn with steel, and that we took them off nightly, they were astounded; their exclamations were many and various.*"[3]

Lucy was particularly struck by the position of women in traditional Kazakh society, noting the difficulties they faced.

"*Do fancy, for a moment, what a position a woman fills. A dog is even considered her superior. When a favourite one is going to have pups, carpets and cushions are given her to lie upon; it is stroked, caressed, and fed upon the best of everything. Woman alone must toil, and they do so very patiently. One Kazakh,*

A lake near the source of the Bascan River

seeing me busy sewing (indeed I was occupied in making a coat for my husband), became so enamoured of my fingers that he asked Mr. Atkinson whether he would be willing to sell me; he decidedly did not know the animal, or he would not have attempted to make the bargain. With me amongst them, there would shortly have been a rebellion in the camp."

Of that, we can have little doubt. On one occasion, when Thomas wanted to sketch, Lucy invited a group of women for tea. They came attired in their best costumes, including a bride wearing her tall, conical *saukele* headdress. The samovar was brought in and tea given out, except to the men present: *"This was the crowning point"*, wrote Lucy. *"The 'lords of the creation' could no longer stand this slight, so arose and made their exit, and I saw no more of them that night. The women appeared to enjoy the fun of the thing."*

Thomas and Lucy's descendants still have the samovar the couple took with them throughout their journeys in Siberia and the Kazakh Steppes. They also have a small fruit knife carried by Lucy throughout her travels.

Having left a Cossack in charge of their baggage they took the other two with them, along with the supplies they would need for an extended stay in the mountains, borne on camels, horses and bulls. Alatau was passed between Thomas and Lucy, depending on the difficulty of the terrain.

After their first overnight camp they awoke to find six inches of snow on the ground in the morning. Later that morning one of the camels fell and was killed. A few hours later some Kazakhs came into their camp to say they had just lost eight horses that had fallen down the mountain, three of them in foal. After a day's delay, during which they decided to switch their baggage to bulls instead of camels, they moved off on horseback to find the elusive verdigris-coloured lake. Once again, they moved high into the mountains where they found an aoul of eight yurts. Sitting on the edge of a steep precipice, far below Lucy could see the beautiful lake. Thomas placed his shotgun besides Lucy and walked off to choose a spot to pitch the tent.

Suddenly, and without apparent explanation, events took a dangerous turn. Lucy looked round to see that one of the Cossacks had been surrounded by men holding sticks. Thomas ran over to help him, only to be confronted by more men carrying sticks – actually yurt poles. Several women too joined in and events appeared to be getting out of hand. Not that Lucy could hear anything; all sound was drowned out by a nearby waterfall. She knew that none of the others were armed. Her first thought was to put down the child and run over with the double-barrelled shotgun, but concerned that Alatau might roll off the cliff in her absence, abandoned the idea. She decided to sit still and see what would happen.

At this point, a second Cossack, who had been with the bulls, came into view. He immediately rode forward, just as a man and two women launched an attack on the first Cossack, who struck one of them. Two men tried to pinion Thomas' arms, but he was too strong for them and broke away. As he did so the second Cossack levelled a rifle. One of the Atkinsons' Kazakh guides now also appeared and drew two pistols from their holsters, cocked and pointed them. No sooner had this happened than everything changed. The men dropped their sticks, doffed their caps and moved back. Lucy, a double-barrelled shotgun over one arm and a baby in the other, walked forward.

By this time, the Cossacks had been able to bind one person from the group, the leader of the aoul, who had led the attack. He had urged his confederates to knock the brains from the strangers and seize their goods, thinking that they were a party of Russians. Thomas asked the Cossacks to release him, but they declined, saying he was still dangerous. After some time, when things had calmed down, Thomas persuaded him to allow two men from the aoul to accompany him and a Cossack to descend to the lake far below. Lucy and Alatau were to stay at the camp, from where she watched Thomas descend through her opera glasses. The leader of the aoul saw the glasses and came over to take a closer look. Lucy was not prepared to take any risks:

"I arose from my seat, determined to show no fear, and stood perfectly still, merely placing my hand in my pocket and grasping my pistol, but without drawing it forth."

The incident seems to have left a strong impression upon Lucy. She noted that they had been just three against 20 or so. *"Amongst this grand mountain scenery I seemed to conceive a more vivid idea of the power and presence of the Deity; and then I felt that the beneficent Being who had called all I saw*

Lucy Atkinson invites a group of Kazakh women to tea

around me into existence, did not neglect to watch and guard even the least of His creatures, if they trusted in Him. What care had been bestowed upon us this very day!"

Just as quickly as the atmosphere had changed earlier, so it changed again. Soon one of the women came over from the aoul, bringing with her a Chinese silk handkerchief with mother-of-pearl decoration, which she presented to the baby Alatau. Lucy, in turn, presented a little red hat she had made for Alatau, to one of the children from the aoul. *"Had I offered a bar of gold it would not have given half the pleasure that this hat did,"* wrote Lucy.

The leader of the attack, now remorseful, killed a sheep with which to honour his guests and when Thomas returned, went forward to shake his hand. He took tea with the Atkinsons and from then on there was no further trouble.

The next day Thomas wanted to go back and sketch the green lake from another angle. Lucy added:

> *"The cause of the peculiar colour of the water we could not ascertain. The lake was about three quarters of a verst wide, and two to two and a half long; and the Kazakhs said it was as deep as the mountain was high, but that we could not believe, though evidently the depth was great. They called it the Jassel-kool, which, translated, means young lake; perhaps a lake newly formed by an earthquake, as the rocks appeared tossed about in great confusion."*

Today the lake is known as Zhasylkul, which contrary to Lucy's interpretation, means Green Lake. Even now it is not easy to reach, as I found out myself in the summer of 2015, when I was able to stand on its shore after a difficult ride on horseback of almost 20 kilometres. Located at an altitude of 1630m, the lake is a beautiful green colour and is fed by mountain streams. In all likelihood it was formed by rocks being jammed into a narrow mountain valley. It is one of the great sights to be seen in the recently opened Djungar Alatau National Park.

For much of this journey through the river valleys of the Djungar Alatau, Thomas and Lucy's guide was a local man, who told them he had once ridden with the great warrior 'Kinsara'. He was referring to Kenisary Kasimov (1802-1847), today regarded as a Kazakh national hero for his resistance to Russian rule.

Kenisary had refused to accept the Russian decision to abolish the title of khan and at one point in the early 1840s had as many as 20,000 horsemen under his command. He was murdered in 1847 by Ormon Khan, a leader of the Kyrgyz tribes, who decapitated him and sent his mummified head to Russia.

The Atkinsons' guide was proud of his association with Kenisary and entertained them with stories of his bold raids and *barantas*. These mountains had often provided protection to Kenisary, as no-one was brave or foolhardy enough to follow him into the trackless valleys and forests. At one point the old guide came across one of the former camp grounds of Kenisary:

> *"He pointed to a place on the north-west side of the valley, near some high precipices, as the locality of the Sultan's yurts. Farther to the west, he indicated the position of the aoul of his band and directed my attention right across the valley to a point near the bank of a torrent, as the spot where the party had always been stationed to guard the pass."*[4]

Not far from this spot, said the guide, the river was swallowed up by a cavern. This in all likelihood refers to the Lepsou River, which disappears underground for a short distance, not far from its source. By darkness Thomas' party was in the exact spot of Kenisary's old encampment.

> *"My guide told me that no one of the band ever dared to disobey his orders, as doing so would have been certain death. He had acquired unbounded power over the minds of his followers by his indomitable courage. If a desperate attack had to be made against fearful odds, he led the van and was ever first in the fight – shouting his war-cry with uplifted battle-axe and plunging his fiery steed into the thickest of the battle. This gave confidence to his men, and was the secret of his success."*[5]

Later, the guide led Thomas to the exact spot where Kenisary had pitched his yurt: *"There were the black ashes of his own hearth; he looked at these for a few minutes and then led the way to the eastwards. As he strode along he often looked back evidently lingering affectionately over a locality that had called up many pleasant recollections."* At the end of several days travelling with the guide Thomas presented him with his fee: two pounds of gunpowder, 50 rifle balls and a small piece of lead, with which the old man was more than delighted.

Lake Zhasylkul, in the Djungar Alatau National Park

Nick Fielding

Thomas describes some remarkable sights in the mountain gorges and valleys, not all of which I have been able to identify. This is still a remote and barely explored region. Vast forests of apples can be found and scientists say this region is the world's most important place for wild apple biodiversity. The cultivated apple (*Malus domestica*) arose in the Tien Shan from the wild apple (*Malus sieversii*) and was spread by bears and other wild ungulates. In the Lepsinsk Valley alone – which I visited in the summer of 2015 – there are 14,000 hectares of wild apple trees of more than 40 varieties.

And besides the trees and wild flowers, the Djungar Alatau remains a wildlife refuge; bears, lynx, wolves, snow leopard, wild boar, maral deer, ibex, wild sheep and many other animals and birds can be found. And until the 1950s this was also the hunting ground for the tiger, tracks of which Thomas and Lucy came across regularly.

Seven days after leaving their Cossack on the banks of the Lepsou, Thomas and Lucy returned to the camp. The Cossack had almost given up hope, believing they were lost forever in the mountains. It was now 2nd July and they decided to follow the Lepsou down to the steppe, visiting an old Kalmuck fortress *en route*. As they made their way to the plains they found many Kazakh aouls, including that of Sultan Boulania, who they had often met in Kapal and who was one of the most senior chieftains on the steppes.

Lucy found the Lepsou River valley to be beautiful and termed it Happy Valley, despite the heat and the swarms of mosquitoes. The heat at this time of the year can reach between 40 and 50 degrees Celsius. Thomas put his rifle down on the sand at one point and received a nasty blister when he tried to pick it up a few minutes later. The mosquitoes were particularly troublesome for Alatau, wrote Lucy:

> "He was one mass of bites. No one could have recognised him. I myself was not much better. I placed the little fellow in bed, perfectly naked, and covered with a piece of muslin, which we contrived to prop up; but still the brutes succeeded in getting in, and it was impossible to sit by and watch the whole time."

In the steppes at the foot of the Alatau Mountains, Thomas and Lucy came across more large groups of Kazakhs moving up

Pippa Smith

Belinda Brown

The Atkinsons' samovar and Lucy's fruitknife

into the summer pastures. They stayed in one aoul consisting of 13 yurts and more than 30 adults, along with thousands of animals. Thomas describes in detail a visit to the aoul of his host Djani-bek by his future son-in-law, who arrived to show off in front of his bride-to-be. At another aoul he was entertained by an old chieftain, one of whose retainers recited epic poetry to entertain them.

> *"Homer was never listened to with more attention than was this shepherd poet, while singing the traditions of the ancestors of his tribe,"* wrote Thomas. *"Whatever power the old Greek possessed over the minds of his audience, was equalled by that of the bard in front of me."*

Thomas was now in his element. One of his main ambitions before reaching the Kazakh steppes had been to travel with the nomads as they moved up to their summer pastures. His portrayal of camp scenes, including the contents of the yurts, the particularities of dress and the methods of animal husbandry are some of the finest ever written about this way of life. He describes this vast mass of animals entering a pass on the way up to the summer pastures: *"The mouth of the pass was about 300 yards wide, between grassy slopes up which it was impossible for either man or animal to climb. The whole width, and as far as I could see, was filled with camels, horses and oxen; Kazakhs were riding among them, shouting and using their whips on any refractory brute that came within their reach. At length we plunged into a herd of horses, with camels in front and bulls and oxen in our rear. We presently passed the grassy slopes to where the gorge narrowed to about 100 yards in width, with precipices rising up on each side to the height of 600 or 700 feet. From this mob of quadrupeds there was no escape on either side and to turn back was utterly impossible, as we were now wedged in among wild horses. These brutes showed every disposition to kick, but fortunately for us, without the power, the space for each animal being too limited. This did not, however, prevent them from using their teeth and it required great vigilance and constant use of the whip to pass unscathed."* [7]

Finally, after many weeks exploring the river valleys and glaciers in the mountains Thomas and Lucy made it to the shores of Alakol lake, which lies just to the north of this part of the Djungar Alatau and marks one of the main entry points into China at the place known as the Djungarian Gate. It was through this region – and the adjoining territory of what is now northern Xinjiang

Nick Fielding

More than 40 different species of apple grow in the Djungar Alatau

or Chinese Djungaria – that the great armies of Genghis Khan moved first into Central Asia before their onward marches to Russia, the Middle East and large parts of Europe.

Thomas and Lucy pitched their tents at the foot of the mountains about an hour or so's ride south of the lake's southern shore. Today, little has changed in the area, except for a few beach huts and the first signs of tourism. You cannot see from one side of the lake to the other, although Piski Island, which has a flock of flamingos, and which was mentioned by Lucy, can easily be seen. She says the Kazakhs used to take their animals over to the island during the winter, when they could cross the ice. She adds that the great geographer Alexander von Humboldt told Thomas in Berlin that he thought there had originally been a volcano in the lake, although Thomas says he found no trace of volcanoes anywhere in Central Asia. The lake has a surface area of over 2650 square kilometres and is salty, although it receives water

A bard entertains a group of Kazakhs on The Steppe

from streams flowing out of the Tarbagatai Mountains.

The stay near the lake was eventful, not least when they were disturbed by intruders in the middle of the night. Lucy was certainly not one to miss out on any action and her account is riveting: "*I always at night placed everything where I could lay my hands upon it at a moment's notice. Placing my husband's pistols and gun into his hands, he started, bidding me lie down and keep quiet, but such was not my nature. If we were to be captured I was determined to see how it was managed, so put on my dressing gown and slippers, and out I went, with my single pistol in my hand; the other had been stolen. It appeared there were about six or eight men; they had come within fifty yards of our tent, but, observing the sentinels, had retreated across a little glen, and rode under the dark shade of a small mountain in front of us.*

"*Our Cossacks, Kazakhs and Mr. Atkinson, mounted their*

horses and rode over the ground, but they were gone; the place afforded many ways of escape, even quite near to us. What appears a vast plain, as level as the hand, when we come to ride over it we find undulating ground, intersected by gullies, where horse and rider may soon be lost to view. It was undoubtedly the intention of these men to have stolen our horses; had they succeeded in doing so, we should have been an easy prey, as without them to have ascended the deep ravine would have been impossible, and the sultry sun and burning sand across the steppe would soon have killed us, to say nothing of the want of water."[8]

At the same time, Lucy seems to have found the place enchanting, describing how she and Thomas sat watching the sun go down over the lake: "*On such nights as these one feels as though living in a land of spirits, everything calm and serene around, not a whisper of any kind. Sometimes a feeling of sadness creeps over one, on thinking that we must once*

Sultan Boulania, "one of the most senior chieftains on the steppes"

more return to the busy world, with all its ceremonies, cares, and troubles; and one would almost wish to be a Kazakh, wandering, like them, amongst all that is beautiful in nature – but then comes the thought that this would be but an idle life."

They found many ancient tombs on the shores of the lake made from sunburnt brick, many of which still remain.

Thomas and Lucy used the camp on the shores of Alakol as a base for their further treks into the mountains. Lucy took part in these journeys and became adept at crossing streams on horseback, including some, she wrote:

"where we had all to ride in together, the one to bear the other up. The Kazakhs, invariably placing me in the centre, and clutching my dress, seemed determined to take care of me. Some of the streams were broad and deep. When it was so, I used to retire behind the reeds

or rocks, as the case might be, and, stripping, put on my bathing gown, with my belt round my waist; and tying my clothing into a bundle, boots and all, I jumped on to my horse – merely holding tight on to him with my legs, there being no saddle – and swam him across in the company of a Kazakh, he gallantly carrying my bundle for me; when I would again retire with my bundle, to re-equip myself." As she noted, *"I am vastly altered since leaving Petersburg."*

It was not until the 26th July that they returned to Alakol for the last time, where once again they faced intruders near the camp, this time four men on horses. A brief skirmish resulted in George, one of the Cossacks, capturing a lance and the pursuit party also found a tethered camel which had been stolen from a neighbouring aoul. Soon they were on the move again, camping close to Sassykol, Alakol's neighbouring lake, where they were tormented by mosquitoes.

Nomadic Kazakhs and their livestock entering a gorge in the Djungar Alatau

On 9th August Thomas and Lucy arrived at a picket close to the Chinese border town of Chougachac, between Alakol and Zaisan lakes and about 700 kilometres from Semipalatinsk. Now known as Tacheng, the town has long been a crossing point between the Kazakh steppes and Chinese Djungaria and is close to the present border crossing at Baktu. The Atkinsons had made the journey despite advice from the Cossacks that they would face imprisonment. From the picket they could see the town in the distance and their intention was to apply for permission to enter. Lucy was struck by the costumes of the officials they met, the first Chinese she had seen on this journey. "*There was no mistaking them and their peculiar costume; their boots were principally of black satin, with very high heels and thick soles; their jackets pleased me amazingly, and were really pretty. Those of the servants were of blue cotton, but their superiors wore silk or satin. The latter is called kanfa, and can be washed exactly like a piece of cotton.*"

An inquiring Chinese border official asked why they wanted to visit the Celestial Empire and Thomas replied that being so near, he merely wanted to pay his respects to the governor and see the town. They were asked to wait for a reply, which would arrive in the evening.

Thomas and Lucy Atkinson, and Alatau meet with Chinese officials

Nothing happened that evening, but the following morning they saw the official party of three officers approaching, together with a military retinue. The border guard insisted that they take Alatau to a meeting with the officials, which took place on a carpet spread beneath some nearby trees. After handshakes and greetings, tea and sweetmeats arrived and, before anything else, the *kalki*, the most senior official, took great delight in picking up Alatau and smothering him with kisses. The officials were very cordial and the scene is portrayed affectionately in a woodcut of Thomas' sketch that appears in Lucy's book..

Conversation was not easy. The Chinese spoke to a Tartar, who then translated their words into Russian to a Cossack, which Lucy in turn translated into English. When Thomas asked if they could enter the town, the official said they were the first English people ever to have visited the region and that the governor would have to obtain special permission from the Emperor.

This would have meant days, if not weeks, of delay and Thomas declined the offer. Lucy then asked if she could go

alone, but the official told her he would likely lose his head for allowing such a visit.

But if Thomas was willing to shave his head and dress as a Tartar, perhaps he would be able to gain entry. Thomas replied that if he could not enter as an Englishman, he would not visit the place at all. Nonetheless, they agreed to share a meal that the officials had brought with them consisting of rice, meat and soup, followed by sweetmeats and then tea. Lucy tried to use chopsticks, whilst the Chinese struggled with spoons and forks. When the time came to depart, Alatau was passed down a long line of soldiers, each of whom embraced him.

With that, Thomas and Lucy decided to press on northwards and made their parting farewells. One of the officials presented Alatau with a large cucumber, which Thomas eyed with relish, having not tasted vegetables for nearly a year. The following day was hard, ten hours riding over burning sand, which affected their eyes and made Lucy very dizzy, but after a night's sleep she was fine again. She emphasises how

Lucy Atkinson can be seen fording a river on horseback in this woodcut from her book

systematic they all were in seeing to their duties once they arrived at a new camp. By now she was a seasoned traveller and even with a small baby, she knew exactly what to do and in which order. For food they relied on flour given to them by the Chinese which they mixed with milk from a Kazakh aoul if they were near one and then fried. Lucy says she was never quite satisfied with food on the steppes:

> *"From the hour of our entering the steppe until we left it, I never knew what it was to have a sufficiency of food; without bread or vegetables it was impossible, at least for me, to feel quite satisfied. Fancy only meat and nothing but meat, then tea without sugar or cream. I was the worst off, having two to nourish; and I can assure you the keen air of the mountains sharpened the little fellow's appetite. One good thing, he had learned to eat meat: he began before he was three months old; at first he ate morsels the size of a pin's head, but bread he did not even know the flavour of."*

She mentions the pleasure of eating apples ("we lived a good deal on them") in those areas where they found them in the mountains.

Somewhere between Chougachac and Ayaguz the Atkinsons came across the aoul of the wealthy Sultan Beck, where Lucy was struck by the beauty of his two daughters.

> *"The youngest was more to my taste, being very pretty; her hair hung in a multitude of braids around her face, and just on the crown of her head she wore quite a coquettish-looking cap. She was slim, and exceedingly graceful in all her movements. Her elder sister was a perfect Amazon."*

Thomas completed a beautiful portrait of the Sultan and his daughters 139, which appears in his first book. He was to visit their aoul again four years later as he travelled south from Djungaria back towards Kapal.

Now Thomas and Lucy were almost on the last leg of their journey. In Ayaguz they exchanged horses for their carriage which had survived their absence for a year. They bade farewell to their Cossack companions with many a tear and headed north to Zmeinogorsk, where they arrived on 3rd September. Not surprisingly, their friends barely recognised them. As Lucy noted: *"Mr. Atkinson was in a terrible plight, his boots had been patched and mended with the bark of trees, till they would scarcely hold together. The first person in request was a bootmaker, whose ingenuity you would find a difficulty in matching. We gave the order for the boots and supplied the man with leather. He looked at Mr. Atkinson's foot, and was going away, when I stopped him, to say he must at once take the measure, as they were required immediately. 'Oh, I never measure,' he replied, and went away: we felt sure the leather would be wasted. In two days they arrived, when my husband declared he had never had a pair of boots fit him so well."*

It was then back to a round of evening parties and cards, which Lucy found intensely boring until she had a go at fortune telling, which proved very popular – and in at least one case, very accurate. And then, after a month's rest, they were off again, heading for Barnaul in the Altai region of Siberia where Thomas intended to spend the winter painting and Lucy in catching up on her reading.

That, of course, was not quite the end of this episode of their adventures. On the first night back in Barnaul, having dined with their old friend Colonel Sokolovsky, they returned to their rooms, which had been heated in their absence due to the freezing conditions outside. In the night Lucy was disturbed by Alatau's laboured breathing and as she attempted to light a candle and get up, found herself almost unable to move and suffering a severe headache. She woke Thomas, who realised what was happening and stumbled towards the door which he pushed open before crashing to the floor where he lay without moving for ten minutes. The oxygen flooded in and they escaped suffocating to death. As soon as they could, they woke all the other residents and then opened thee stove, to find it was still burning and consuming all the oxygen in the room. *"Had the child not fortunately awakened me, I make no doubt that it would have been our last sleep"*, wrote Lucy.

It was the end of an extraordinary 18 months of Lucy's life. From a governess in an aristocratic family in cosmopolitan St Petersburg, she had married, become pregnant, travelled thousands of miles with her new husband, nearly died of thirst and of cold, delivered a baby under the most extreme of circumstances, ridden on horseback into some of the most remote mountain valleys in the world up to altitudes approaching 3,000 metres, faced robbers intent on murdering them in their beds and become friends with some of the great characters and leaders of the Kazakh hordes. Nothing like this had ever been achieved by a woman traveller before. And this was only the start. Another four years would go by before Lucy and Thomas returned to St Petersburg. The adventure had barely begun.   ∎

---

1. The seven rivers of the Semirechye region are: the Ili, Karatal, Bean, Acsou, Sarcan, Bascan and Lepsou. Thomas visited them all.

2. *Recollections*, op cit, p150

3. Ibid, p154

4. *Amoor*, op cit, p221

5. Ibid, p223

Sultan Beck with his family, camels and hunting eagle

Mountainscape in Kazakhstan

Chapter
NINE

A BRIEF RETURN

In 1852, three years after returning from Kapal, Thomas – this time alone, as Lucy was in Irkutsk in eastern Siberia – ventured back to Semirechye in Eastern Kazakhstan. He arrived in the early autumn from Djungaria, having completed a formidable ride south from Irkutsk, across the top of Mongolia, then south-west through Djungaria to the Barluk Mountains in between the Tarbagatai and the Djungar Alatau ranges. He had been directed to the aoul of Sultan Ishonac Khan, who received him in peace and the following day provided eight of his followers to protect Thomas as he rode westwards towards the Tarbagatai Mountains, just to the north of Lake Alakol – a journey of between four and six days.

The Kazakhs were armed and when Thomas asked why he was told that in this inhospitable region there were bands of robbers known as *Byjarat*, who were a mixture of Kazakh bandits and Chinese who had escaped from the penal colonies on the Ili River to the south. Much of the route was across a sandy steppe, with barely a blade of grass evident. Dust thrown up by the horses as they rode over salt pans in this desert made the riders incessantly thirsty. A large lake they came across held only brackish water, which nonetheless the horses drank. Only when they reached a river the following morning could they quench their thirst.

Soon they were passing to the north of the border town of Chougachac, where Alatau had so entertained the border officials three years previously. From here they rode west and then south into the Tarbagatai Mountains.

By the evening they had reached the aoul of Sultan Yanantuck, who had arrived three days previously and whose ancestral lands these were. High conical tombs, which you can still find today, marked the places where his ancestors were buried. Each year, for a week, his family would visit the spot and remember their ancestors. Here also were numerous large *kurgans*.

A large tomb in the Tarbagatai Mountains

Nick Fielding

A modern Kazakh tomb on the steppe near the Tarbagatai Mountains

Thomas was particularly taken by Sultan Yanantuck, saying that he and his family were by far the most intelligent people he had met on the steppes. As with the previous aoul in which he had stayed, the Sultan provided eight riders to accompany Thomas, while his former outriders headed back towards Djungaria.

The following day Thomas was once again on the move, heading south towards the Alatau Mountains. Soon they were in sight of Alakol, but even so there was little water or grass. "*The only living things we found were scorpions and tarantulas – bad food for a dinner*," wrote Thomas.[1] The difficulty they now faced was negotiating a route between Alakol and the neighbouring lakes, through almost impenetrable reedbeds. Kazakhs at an aoul told them they would have to swim some broad and deep places and they provided two men to show the route, without whom such a journey through the reeds and rushes would have been impossible. During the Soviet era a ferry used to run, but when we attempted to follow the route in the summer of 2015, we were told that it was no longer in operation.

In the end Thomas had to strip down, put all his sketches and weapons into bags and then swim across open water. Three times they had to do this before they made it to the shore of Alakol. Now they turned towards the west in search of the aoul of Sultan Beck, whom Thomas had visited in 1849. They arrived late and had to awake him from his slumbers, which might explain his bad-tempered response to them, sending them a diseased sheep for dinner, which Thomas quickly returned with a curt message saying that even though the sultan had such a large body he had the heart of a mouse. After a stand-off the Sultan relented and sent over two girls with a more acceptable animal, saying that it was one of the best from his flock and that he would visit Thomas shortly, which he did. All difficulties were forgotten and a bard was summoned to perform heroic songs. The following morning the sultan provided ten horsemen to accompany Thomas to the south-west towards the aoul of Sultan Boulania, another of the Kazakhs he had met in 1849.

They headed for the Lepsou River which runs into the featureless steppes between the Alatau Mountains and Lake Balkash and arrived at Boulania's aoul, who wrote him a passport that would be good for any of the tribal leaders in the Middle Horde and two of the leaders of the Great Horde.

Thomas was now, once again, following the old Cossack road – or more properly the Old China Road, for it had been in use for millennia; Friar William Rubruck had passed this way on his way to the Mongol court at Karakorum, as had Buddhist missionaries and even before them, Nestorian Christians, who had followers on the banks of Lake Issyk Kul in Kyrgyzstan.

Thomas' next host was Sultan Alic Iholdi, who claimed descent from Timour Khan. He carried a remarkable chair with him from aoul to aoul, complete with peacock feathers at each corner, as well as a huge iron cauldron for cooking sheep.

Now they were approaching what Thomas always refers to as the Karatau – an outlying ridge that marks the southern edge of the Kazakh steppes, leaving a wide valley between there and the main Alatau chain. The name seems to have disappeared in modern usage. Four more days of riding, much of it across arid steppes, criss-crossed by deep ravines and morasses, brought them to the aoul of Thomas' old friend, Sultan Souk. The old man was now 80 years old, well past his prime, but still an imposing figure. Even if he could not take part in barantas, he could still help plan them.

Souk himself, along with nine of his people, accompanied Thomas on the next leg of his journey, this time south towards the Alatau. They parted at an old Kalmuck tomb, Souk heading to a tribal gathering for horse-racing and wrestling, while Thomas headed towards the River Balikty and from there up a gorge towards the Alatau Mountains and a gorge known as Tchim-Boulac (pure spring).

Thomas spent some time sketching here, noting the large basalt columns and the cliffs made from porphyry and jasper. He was now west of Kapal, close to the western-most point of the Djungar Alatau, and was soon approaching the point where the Kora River breaks out of the mountains to join two other rivers at what is now the city of Tekeli and to become the Karatal River, which flows into Lake Balkash, which Thomas glimpsed from the mountain slopes. He had to leave his horse at the mouth of the Kora gorge and walk up this steep-sided valley. "*We had to climb over huge masses of rock, some we were obliged to creep under, they being much too high to climb over – in other places, plants were growing in tropical luxuriance. A scramble of five hours brought me to a point I could not pass; her the rocks rose quite perpendicularly from*

The old China Road running along the base of the Djungar Alatau Mountains

Vladimir Gostyevski

the boiling flood, making ascent to the summit impossible."[2] To this day the gorge at this point remains inaccessible due to the steepness of its sides.

After a hard day's walking Thomas returned to his yurt, where a sheep was being cooked in a cauldron and camels and horses were close by. *"Tired as I was, I could not resist sketching the scene, which will ever be impressed upon my memory, as well as the splendid sunset over the steppe."* Sadly, the whereabouts of this sketch, like so many others out of more than 100 painted by Thomas in the Kazakh steppes and Alatau Mountains, remains unknown.

From Tekeli, Thomas rode back towards Kapal, making one particularly dramatic sketch of falls on the River Kapal in the mountains above the town. He again visited the Tamchiboulac Spring in the town of Kapal, but does not mention the town or its inhabitants. He also visited the warm springs at Arasan,

which were first commercialised as a health resort in the 1880s. They are classified as weakly radioactive and weakly sulphate-chloride-natrium thermal springs. The temperature of the majority of springs is 35-37C.

By the time of this second visit, Kapal was already beginning to expand. Thomas notes in *Oriental and Western Siberia* that its *"aspect has been completely changed"* and that its population had reached 11,000. There was a large community of Tartar merchants busily engaged in trade with both the nomadic tribes and also with China. *"Such has been the sudden rise of Kapal, its prosperity had induced the people to form another settlement on the Almaty, or 'Apple River', about 200 miles south-west of the former fort,"* he writes. He must have still been in touch with someone in the town who had passed on this information prior to the publication of the book in 1858. Semyon Tienshansky and the great Kazakh explorer Chokan Valikhanov had

The gorge of the Tchim-Boulac

Falls on the River Kapal

both visited the town by then and an artist travelling with Tienshansky had made a sketch of the town, which shows the extent to which it had expanded.

Thomas foretold the end of the nomadic way of life, pointing to the practicality of the Cossack settlers, who would soon dominate the local economy. And, in what may be one of the very first passages to express the sentiments that later underpinned the idea of the Great Game in Central Asia, he recommended that Britain should consider transporting its manufactured goods from India, across the Himalayas to this new market. "*The distance to Vernoje[3] and Kapal is about one third of that from these places to the great fair on the Volga. This is of no small importance commercially, as these towns will become the centres whence the Tatar merchants will send forth their agents to disperse their goods among the Kazakhs of the steppes. From these points they will also go to the Mongolian tribes on the north of the Gobi and this region contains a vast population. I have no doubt, should this trade be established, that the merchandise will find its way through the country of the Kalkas into Daouria and to the regions behind the Selenga and the sources of the Amoor, where it may advantageously compete with goods brought up the latter river.*"[4]

Russia, of course, would never allow British influence to grow in Central Asia and British imperial statesmen in turn became obsessed with the idea that the Russians would not stop moving south until they were on the banks of the Indus itself. Anglo-Russian diplomacy for the next 70 years was dominated by the Great Game, which began almost as soon as the tribes of the steppes had been pacified.

From Kapal, Thomas tells us he travelled back towards Ayaguz, leaving the Alatau region after a stay of 123 days. A ride of 17 days from Alakol brought him to Semipalatinsk and the Russian frontier, from where he returned to Irkutsk – and Lucy and Alatau. No more would he travel on the Kazakh steppes, although the preponderance of drawings from this region and the number of pages he devoted in both his books to his stay there shows that it forever held a place in his heart. It would be another five years before he returned to England and published his first book. This was received with great acclaim and Thomas was soon a prominent figure in the salons of London, where his pictures sold rapidly and soon decorated some of the grandest houses in the land. But within three years of his return, at the age of 61, Thomas had died, broken by the exertions of years of travel in extremes of heat and cold. That, however, was far from the end of the story… ■

1. OWS, op cit, p560.
2. Ibid, p573-4
3. Vierney, or Almaty
4. OWS, op cit, p293.

Sketch of Kapal made in 1857, with
the Cossack bastion on the right

Sultan Alie Iholdi (centre) with his son and wife

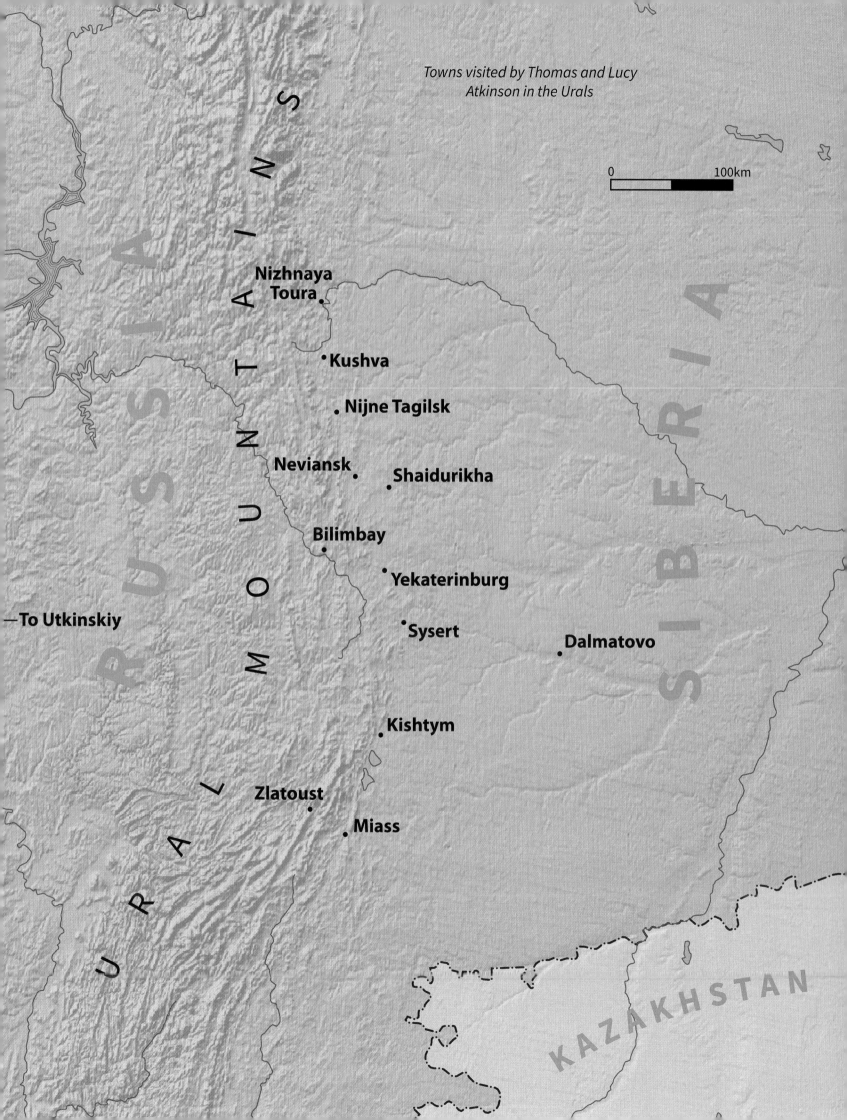

Towns visited by Thomas and Lucy
Atkinson in the Urals

0   100km

U R A L S

R U S S I A

S I B E R I A

U R A L   M O U N T A I N S

**Nizhnaya
Toura**

Kushva

Nijne Tagilsk

Neviansk

Shaidurikha

Bilimbay

Yekaterinburg

—**To Utkinskiy**

Sysert

Dalmatovo

Kishtym

Zlatoust

Miass

K A Z A K H S T A N

RUSSIA

Barnaul

Lake
Teletskoye

Kolyvan

Zmeinogorsk

Semipalatinsk

Ridder

Altai Mountains

Ust Kamenogorsk

Zyrianovsk

Mt Bielukha

KAZAKHSTAN

MONGOI

Kokpekty

CHINESE
DJUNGARIA

Lake
Zaisan

Ayakoz

Tarbagatai
Mountains

Lake
Sassykol

Lake Balkhash

Lake
Alakol

CHINA

Lepsinsk

Zhansugurov   Sarqan

Arasan

Kopal

Djungar Alatau Mountains

Tekeli

*The Altai Mountains and the
Semirechye region of Eastern Kazakhstan*

0   100km

Lake
Issy Kol

KYRGYZSTAN

Afterword

Thomas and Lucy's arrival back in Barnaul in the late autumn of 1849, along with their baby boy Alatau, was not the end of their travels. For the next four summers they continued to explore remote areas in eastern Siberia, Mongolia and Central Asia. In May the following year, for example, they left Barnaul and spent the summer travelling to Irkutsk close the Lake Baikal in Eastern Siberia. In May 1851 they left Irkutsk for the mountains in the north, returning to Irkutsk in September. In May 1852 Lucy travelled back to Barnaul by carriage, whilst Thomas took a different route on horseback via Mongolia, Djungaria and the Great Steppe. In February 1853 they left Barnaul together for Ekaterinburg and spent the summer in the Ural Mountains. Not until 24th December 1853 did they arrived back in St Petersburg.

During the harsh Siberian winters the Atkinsons stayed either in Barnaul or Irkutsk, where Thomas painted watercolours from the sketches he had made throughout his journeys. He completed around 560 sketches and paintings, although the whereabouts of only a small fraction of these is known. Some were certainly destroyed in a house fire at the home of his grandson, ALC 'Jack' Atkinson in Hawaii in 1922. Others were probably left in Russia and have since disappeared. Yet more are doubtless hanging in some of England's grand houses, bought directly from him in London or at the auctions that followed his death.

Soon after the Atkinsons arrived back in St Petersburg the Crimean War broke out and it is remarkable that the Atkinsons chose not to return to England at that point. We know that Thomas sought and received permission to stay on in Russia to complete his paintings. He was given assurances that he and his family would be protected and they settled into life in the Russian capital. It is hardly surprising that Thomas dedicated his first book to Tsar Alexander II, who had become Emperor in 1855 following the death of his father Nicholas I. Undoubtedly it was Lucy's connections to the highest ranks of the Russian aristocracy that smoothed the path for this exceptional permission – no less important than the granting of Thomas' passport in 1846.

The Atkinsons eventually arrived back in England in 1858 and the publication of Thomas' first book was a huge success. He was soon made a Fellow of the Royal Geographical Society, the Geological Society and the Ethnographic Society. A second book followed in 1860, but already Thomas was not well. Now 61, his health was rapidly failing. In August 1861 he died, leaving Lucy with a 12-year-old boy and no income. Worse was to come. Thomas's first wife, Rebecca, who appears to have been unaware of her former husband's return, now came forward to claim his estate – or what little there was.

With no income, Lucy was in severe financial difficulties. Her book, published in 1863, would have provided a small income. She was also granted a government pension of £100 and a public subscription organised through the RGS raised enough money to send Alatau to Rugby School. After that we hear little more about her. A few letters have turned up suggesting she may have returned to Russia and it is known that she died in London in 1893, aged 75.

As for Alatau, after leaving Rugby, he became a journalist in Newcastle-upon-Tyne and then a teacher at Durham School. From there, in 1869 he and his wife and baby daughter emigrated to Hawaii, where he soon made a mark, setting up a school and editing the Hawaiian Gazette. He became director of education for the islands and organised their first census, in the process becoming a staunch advocate of American annexation. The full story will have to wait for another occasion.

Already the reader will have realised that the Atkinsons were not run-of-the-mill, nineteenth century travellers. There are many books written by people who travelled by post-roads across Asia in those years. Some of them are interesting, others less so. But the Atkinsons were different. Although they cannot be described as 'scientific' explorers, their books are full of remarkable insights and geographical and ethnographic observations that stand the test of time. They offer the only detailed description of life on the Great Steppe in the mid-nineteenth century. Hopefully this book will re-introduce this remarkable couple to a wider public and help to restore them to their rightful place in the history of exploration. ∎

Acknowledgements

It was my good friend the bookdealer Toby English who in drawing my attention to a signed first edition of Thomas Atkinson's book *Oriental and Western Siberia*, first got me interested in this story. Soon after, he found me a copy of Thomas' second book, which I also bought. So it is to Toby, who sadly died in 2015, that I offer my first thanks. Without him, this book would never have been written.

I very quickly realised that Thomas and Lucy's story was an untold epic and decided to begin the process of research, to uncover what lay behind the remarkable events of their lives. That eventually led me to contact Sally Hayles, who was busily engaged in organising an exhibition of Barnsley artists, including Thomas Atkinson. Through Sally, I made contact with three other women who have all contributed enormously to my understanding of the Atkinsons: Marianne Simpson in Australia is a direct descendant of one of Lucy Atkinson's brothers; Susanna Hoe is an Oxford-based author, whose book Travels in Tandem includes a chapter on the Atkinsons; and Patricia Polansky is the Russian Bibliographer at the University of Hawaii's Hamilton Library in Honolulu. To all four of them I owe an enormous debt of gratitude for all the work they have put in to revealing the story of Thomas and Lucy.

I am also deeply grateful to Thomas and Lucy's descendants, who have without exception been helpful and put up with my questions over the years and have turned out without fail for public events. In particular, I would like to thank Paul and Charlene Dahlquist of Big Island, Hawaii for accommodating me and my wife Ros in 2015 during a wonderful research trip to Hawaii where I also had the opportunity to give a talk at the school founded by Alatau, Thomas and Lucy's son. Thank you also for allowing me to view invaluable family papers. Pippa Smith and her family and Belinda Brown and her family could not have been more helpful.

I could not have achieved anything in two fantastic trips to Kazakhstan without the brilliant support and translation skills of Vladimir Gostyevski. Thanks also to everyone at the Kazakh Geographic Society, particularly to director Nurlan Abduov, for making my first trip to Kazakhstan so successful. In London thanks also to Gauhar Bramley-Fenton of the British-Kazakh Society for making that trip happen. Thanks too to Yergali-Ata, a man with an encyclopaedic knowledge of Kapal and its history.

Amongst others I would like to thanks are: Caroline Lam, librarian at the Geological Society; Eugene Ray, Janet Turner and other library staff of the Royal Geographical Society who now look after Thomas Atkinson's diaries; Alasdair Macleod, head of Enterprise and Resources at the RGS; David McClay, John Murray Archive Curator, National Library of Scotland; Dr Ekaterina Rogatchevskaia, Lead East European Curator (Russian), European Studies, British Library; Katrin Rauhut, Albert-Ludwigs-Universität, Freiburg; Sarah Walpole, Archivist and Photo Curator, Royal Anthropological Institute; Professor John Diemer, UNC Charlotte; Dr Christine McCulloch Senior Visiting Research Associate, School of Geography and the Environment, University of Oxford; Jonathan Makepeace, Imaging Services Manager, British Architectural Library, Royal Institute of British Architects; Rachel Cornes, Museums Manager, Tameside MBC; Maria Singer, Imaging and Rights Assistant, Yale Center for British Art; Sierra Dixon, Research and Collections Associate, Connecticut Historical Society; Andrew Brown, Collection Online Cataloguer (Books), the Royal Collection; Virginia Mills, Project Officer, Joseph Hooker Correspondence Project, The Royal Botanic Gardens, Kew; Kathi Stanley, Manuscripts and Special Collections, New York State Library; Susan Palmer, FSA, Archivist and Head of Library Services, Sir John Soanes Museum; Georgina Tom, Archivist, 'Iolani School, Honolulu; Dr Jin Noda, Waseda University, Tokyo; William St-Clair; Barry Jackson of the Cawthorne Victoria Jubilee Museum; Helen Price, Special Collections Team Assistant, Brotherton Library, University of Leeds; Lyn Crawford, Archivist, RBS Archives; Professor William Fierman, Dept of Central Eurasian Studies, Indiana University; Professor Meruert Abusseitova in Almaty; and Elena Sergeevna Selina at the V I Surikov Museum in Krasnoyarsk. My good friends Andrei Soldatov and Irina Borogan in Moscow have always been on hand to offer help, translations and advice. Natalya Volkova of Barnaul has been a wonderful correspondent and has managed to publish a Russian-language edition of Lucy's book, which is a great achievement. Ben Phillips and Julia Leikin also helped with research and translations in Russia.

I would like to offer a special thanks to His Excellency, Mr Erzhan Kazykhanov, Ambassador Extraordinary and Plenipotentiary of the Republic of Kazakhstan to the United Kingdom of Great Britain, who has taken a personal interest in the story of Thomas and Lucy Atkinson and who was kind enough to address my lecture at the Royal Asiatic Society in December 2014. Thanks are also due to other staff at the Embassy in London, including Mr Askar Zhiymbayev. My humblest apologies if I have omitted thanks to any of the many people who have been so generous with their time and expertise.

Thanks too, to Rupert Goodman, Marie-Claire Patin, Jon Deane and Eamonn Daly at FIRST for making this book happen, and to my agent, Robert Kirby of United Agents.

Finally, I offer my heartfelt thanks and deepest love to my wife Rosamund, who not only has put up with my all-consuming interest in the Atkinsons for some years, but on several occasions has even consented to travel with me to Central Asia. I could not ask for more.